# BIG DATA MEETS LITTLE DATA:

## BASIC HADOOP TO ANDROID AND ARDUINO WITH THE CLOUD, SAS, AND APACHE OPEN SOURCE

By

### Keith Allan Jones, Ph.D.

www.qualimaticpress.com

1

© 2015 by Keith Allan Jones, Ph.D.

Jones, Keith Allan

Big Data Meets Little Data: Basic Hadoop to Android and Arduino with the Cloud, SAS and Apache Open Source / Keith Allan Jones (Bibliography and Appendix with sub-category index).

ISBN-13: 978-1512099003
ISBN-10: 1512099007

1. Computers. 2. Systems Architecture. 3. Distributed Systems and Computing. I. Title: Basic Hadoop to Android and Arduino with the Cloud, SAS and Apache Open Source (First Edition)

# DEDICATION

This book is dedicated to all the contributors to the Apache Open Source Project, from many academic and free trade entrepreneurs, as well as many web innovators from Facebook, Google, Twitter, Yahoo, and others, including SAS, IBM, and Microsoft; as their contributions have helped build a better world.

## TABLE OF CONTENTS

# FIGURES

# CODE EXAMPLES

# CHAPTER 1

# INTRODUCTION AND BACKGROUND

SAS® has been an early leader in Big Data technology architecture to more easily integrate across system platforms for development of processes based on improvement of Apache Open Source projects for Hadoop and MapReduce, Cassandra, and other Big Data platforms.

During this same time there have been other very seminal technologies emerging – based on the new Arduino microprocessor hardware and IDE, and smart cell phone applications, which involve multi-sensor slave integration to a single master node for data acquisition pre-processing and output to local storage – or even wireless data streaming to HDFS remote file systems using Hadoop.

Options to bridge Big Data Hadoop to Arduino, Android or other Little Data technologies using SAS® are highlighted, but there are many smart app foundation platforms from IBM, SAP, Oracle, and others, as well as new Cloud services from Google, Amazon and Microsoft.

11

These vendor platforms can also provide many of the core foundations for Big Data. This book focuses on history and summarization of the foundations of Big Data technology SAS® solutions, for Little Data Integration to and from Android and Arduino and other micro-platforms for apps that can be managed by DI Studio and DataFlux.

Technology to bridge many large warehouses and data marts to disparate small files from single point of Data Integration is not new to SAS – which has always been able to handle massive source file data management versus integration to many small files or tables – from early days of SAS for IBM mainframes, and products like MXG to analyze MVS with SMF and RMF logs.

Many of the SAS products used in the past are similar to Big Data today – as Thomas Edison was to say:

### *"All Big progress comes from Little improvements"*.

Big Data Hadoop has been one of the most popular emerging new technologies for nearly a decade, and has been implemented at most of the world's largest organizations. Yet, within the recent past, it has been the focus of criticism due to the difficulty to develop, configure and maintain, especially with regard to the MapReduce, Cassandra and the more advanced Apache foundations.

These are the traditional trade-offs of 'free' Open Source versus major vendor enhanced platforms: 1) such Open Source can be modified in-house, but then it must be maintained in-house; and 2) there is no 'guarantee' or any significant testing, which is a major benefit of vendor platforms, which provide standards and 'freeze' releases.

The new Apache Hadoop 2.0 foundation provides some new utility tools to address this, as well as several leading Cloud service API's; but SAS DI Studio and DataFlux are more extensible solutions (which are generally matched by other big vendors such as IBM, MS, and SAP).

Also, the new Apache Hadoop 2.0 'layer' platform libraries and specific Big to Small application systems are appropriate for many small organizations with limited IT resources who are willing to trade-off the risk; but for most larger organizations, major vendors such as SAS (and also IBM, Microsoft, SAP, Oracle, Teradata and others) are a more appropriate technology strategy – especially if these major vendors are already a significant part of the existing and legacy IT infrastructure.

In this book, SAS examples are provided as representative of Gartner Quadrant for 'Best of Class' major vendor Big Data; but each of the other major vendors have similar product offerings of each of the categories presented here, and each can be compared with regard to specific functionality, as rated by Gartner, Forrester or other leading IT industry rating organizations.

For this book, which is specifically to address not only Big Data concepts, but also concepts related to its increasingly desirable integration to 'Little Data' (which is a newer set of technologies – where automated data feeds to local or remote Cloud servers from smart phones such as Android or microprocessors such as Arduino – often include data gaps which benefit from statistical imputation).

As such, SAS Statistical Analysis Systems are widely recognized worldwide as being the leading academic statistical software, provide cutting edge platforms and products that can be most easily adapted and implemented into a reliable management platform for Big to Little Data integration. There are other highly rated major vendors for Big to Little Data integration, including IBM (since their acquisition of SPSS, the leading competitor to SAS); as well as many other major Big Data vendors who are adding analytics and statistical software to support Little Data, including Microsoft in SQL Server SSAS and Data Mining add-ons, and SAP, Oracle, Teradata – as well as many web visualization platforms now providing similar advanced analytics, such as Tableau, QlikView and Tibco Spotfire.

Also relevant in the emerging growth of major vendor products and services to provide such Big Data to Little Data integrated data management that can be readily configured (based on the system data integration software of SAS, IBM and others), must also include the emerging major Data Cloud vendors – from Microsoft, Amazon and Google, as well as many other smaller vendors who are increasingly offering similar but scaled down services at lower price points. These are also covered in this book.

In addition, this book will cover examples from R language as one more alternative to write code to support simple implementations of Big Data (as well as equivalent code in SAS Base and Data Step programming – as R project Open Source is now the most common statistical programming language taught in universities – yet the SAS free University Edition software remains a leading favorite). Other languages Open Source language such as Python are also emerging, but R libraries are more extensible and it is generally the view of Gartner, Forrester and others that R is the leading language for integration to SAS for imputations.

After review of the basic concepts of Big Data Hadoop and MapReduce, to Small Data (including File Federation services related to Cassandra, as well as the high speed web search optimization innovations of Google, Yahoo, Twitter and others); the major focus of this book is to focus on just a few of the many emerging code libraries to support integrated architecture for applications based on Arduino microprocessor nodes and Android as well as other smart cell phone platform apps.

Most of these Arduino and Android class apps are coded in variations of C and C++ language, including both native C as well as proprietary interpreter and scripting languages with 'compile-build' tools for implementation and deployment – and also will be covered by review of examples in this book – as they related to basic concepts and examples of applications using both Arduino and Android IDE and API libs for Big to Little Data coding.

This book is written primarily for both advanced Big Data and Data Scientists using SAS, as well as new or intermediate Data Scientists who use SAS. It is largely focused on the use of DI Studio with Data Quality Management from new DataFlux options – as well as SAS DI Studio and other Enterprise BI tools to support newly emerging Open Source versions of Apache HDFS, Cassandra, and MapReduce standards that are supported by the leading Big Data and Cloud vendors (which can all be managed by the SAS Enterprise BI products) capable to support data integration to Arduino, Android and other Little Data platforms.

This includes new ways to bridge data acquisition from sub-miniature Arduino microprocessor boards via

Direct Wire, Wireless, RF, IR, Ethernet, and Personal Area Network node linkage to new Web Cloud services as well ways to 'burn' EEPROM" code with statistical models for mass production of software and hardware apps.

This will begin with a summary of Big Data foundations and history, with most relevant aspects of both original and current concepts of Small Data (which is not often understood as much as Big Data); then elaborate to explain Little Data to introduce SAS programmers and analysts to many new opportunities.

This begins with a general background of Hadoop for SAS Big Data to Small Data configurations, and continues to importance of MapReduce and remote Cloud services – including Federated file services – which are critical to dynamic management of large numbers (or even changing numbers) of input files.

Then some examples of Little Data apps, based on Arduino, Android, and related platforms, are presented as an introduction for SAS programmers and analysts interested to experiment with custom sensor log data and prototype near-realtime data acquisition and message streaming services that can be integrated to Big Data and Cloud services using SAS DI Studio, SAS Data Federation Server and SAS BI platforms.

Finally some examples of leading SAS vendor user group code, as well as examples of related Open Source free domain code related to and useful to programmers and technologists (along with web links for blogs and resources to monitor, and offer your own support are presented later in this book). Now we will begin a review of some basic concepts of Big Data Hadoop and MapReduce.

CHAPTER 2


# BIG DATA HADOOP AND MAP REDUCE


As Hadoop and MapReduce technology matures to its second decade, it is used as an essential part of the IT infrastructure of nearly half of the Fortune 500, and continues to grow as its performance improves. There have been hundreds of independent benchmark performance studies conducted (including by SAS), which consistently demonstrate following typical comparative load time-resource ratios:

- Hadoop HDFS processes file loads between 15% to 25% faster with less resources than RDBMS

- Star Schema RDBMS loads process data between 40% to 50% faster than traditional RDBMS

- Star Schema Hadoop HDFS loads process data 80% to 90% faster than traditional RDBMS

Cost reductions and performance gains for RDBMS conversions to Star Schema configurations are very good – but gains from conversions of traditional RDBMS to Hadoop with Star Schemas are very great. Such cost reductions and performance gains are complex, yet are largely familiar to SAS users due to over two decades of SAS technology innovations related to parallel, scalable and grid processing by SAS.

The capabilities of SAS to provide both basic and advanced Big Data solutions include SAS/BASE implementations of Hadoop and HDFS foundations that are supported by the SASReduce macro library as developed by SAS consultant David Moors at White Hound Ltd. In UK – which includes the SAS invocation macro as shown below, which uses syntax familiar to SAS Macro programmers for HDFS:

```
%if &sysscp = 'WIN' %then %do;
    systask command "filesplit -s
    &fpath&fname 65536"
    taskname=splitfile
    status=splitstat wait;
    waitfor _all_ splitfile;
%end;
%else do;
    systask command "split -bytes=64M
    &fpath&fname chunk"
    taskname=splitfile
    status=splitstat wait;
    waitfor _all_ splitfile;
%end;
```

This SASReduce process invocation code is part of a much larger SAS Base code library cited at the end of this book. SASReduce is compliant to Apache Open Source specifications. This and several emerging Hadoop HDFS and MapReduce libraries based on the original Google extensions, which can all be registered as metadata and integrated into SAS DI Studio and DataFlux by User Defined Functions for Big Data Hadoop, Small Data Federation Mapping, and both Android and Arduino Little Data app sketches described later. The basic methods of Google MapReduce extensions to Hadoop can be summarized from sample NASA web log data Moors presented at SAS Global Forum 2014 to demonstrate SASReduce are shown in Figure 1 below:

```
199.72.81.55 - - [01/Jul/1995:00:00:01 -0400] "GET
/history/apollo/ HTTP/1.0" 200 6245
205.212.115.106 - - [01/Jul/1995:00:00:12 -0400] "GET
/shuttle/countdown/countdown.html HTTP/1.0" 200 3985
d104.aa.net - - [01/Jul/1995:00:00:13 -0400] "GET
/shuttle/countdown/ HTTP/1.0" 200 3985
129.94.144.152 - - [01/Jul/1995:00:00:13 -0400] "GET / HTTP/1.0"
200 7074
d104.aa.net - - [01/Jul/1995:00:00:15 -0400] "GET
/shuttle/countdown/count.gif HTTP/1.0" 200 40310
```

**Figure 1. NASA Web Log Truncate and Keyword Data from SASReduce Demo from Moors (2014)**

Basically, Apache Hadoop Open Source applies two very simple principles that go back to the earliest computer technologies:

1) <u>try to keep the major bulk of processing centralized to a single location</u> of servers or processors in order to avoid network bottlenecks; and

2) <u>try to standardize and minimize control data into small blocks</u> or sets of map pointers that are efficiently standardized to optimize access.

There are also many other Big Data and Hadoop methods for analysis of vast data source files with rapid data reduction algorithms, as well as file size and process speed optimizations, and server process localizations, but most involve a simple range of processing that combines the following:

- A <u>truncation</u> approach which scans only first _N_ bytes (usually 20 to 120), as in system logs to extract strings for URL's and date/time values to link to table values for statistical summaries

- A <u>keyword</u> based scan approach within a file to extract hit or incidence counts as a percent of total occurs within files, for comparisons to rank context and content versus a text corpora archive

All significant products or platforms for Big Data are based predominantly upon the two most important creative new innovations by Apache Open Source project within the past decade are shown in Figure 2

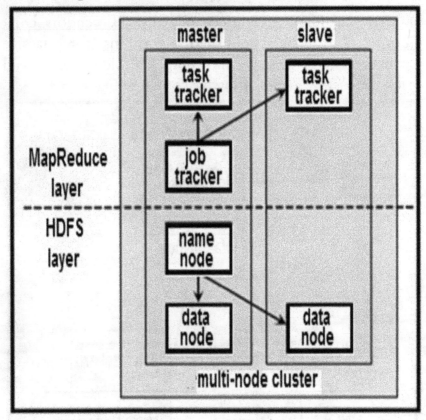

**Figure 2. Big Data Hadoop HDFS and MapReduce as Originally Defined by Apache Open Source Project**

These innovations to Big Data included both many Open Source contributor enhancements of academic supporters to Apache Hadoop project, as well as first major vendors:

21

1) <u>Apache Hadoop free modifiable Open Source</u> LIB's, including Hadoop Distributed File System, MapReduce, Hive, PigLatin language, and related innovations; and

2) <u>Many small Open Source and large IT vendors copy</u> **Google** <u>MapReduce published algorithms</u> for massive parallelization, to achieve maximum scalable system speed at lowest cost by load sharing (as shown in Figure 3).

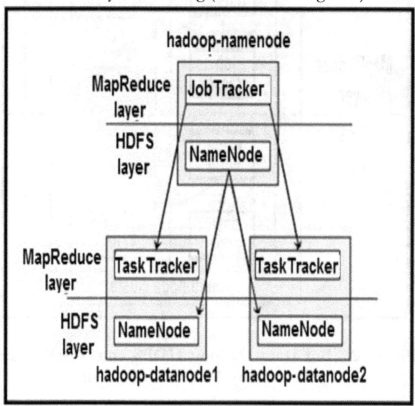

**Figure 3. Expansion of Big Data MapReduce and for Web Search Engine Optimization per Google**

Such HDFS are file systems which can be configured as master-slave servers across local and/or remote internet servers, which involve one JobTracker on a master host server, and multiple TaskTracker nodes on each server and/or application domain, with polling of remote node on a regular basis.

The default Hadoop JobTracker allocates to the TaskTracker server nearest to the data.

If one TaskTracker is very slow, it can delay the entire MapReduce job until the slowest job finishes successfully or fails due to overloads or errors. Google was first to apply such MapReduce to web search optimization.

By default Apache Hadoop Open Source uses FIFO from a stack of task processes, as a very simple time-based queue process scheduler.

This simple scheduler did not account for any conditional controls for changing process priorities, and as a result, two lead web giants developed two leading innovations:

1)   **Fair Scheduling**: The fair scheduler was first developed by **Facebook** (in fact, this was among several algorithms that were highlighted in the movie "***The Social Network***" in 2010 about Mark Zuckerberg and chronicles famously contested in lawsuits from his early collaborators – and was part of the 'tests' presented to early FB hires).

The 'Fair Scheduler' was designed to optimize response times for small jobs within a larger application jobstream.

This innovation had three basic characteristics:

a) jobstreams are grouped into task resource pools;

b) each pool has a minimum starting share of the combined resources available from  main server and slave servers; and

c) available resources in each cluster server node send messaging back to the main server on a sampling schedule that can be set by Hadoop and MapReduce configuration parameters, as well as specifications on how to split current unused cpu and storage capacity among all servers defined as process clusters.

Concurrent to the early major innovations to Big Data and Hadoop and MapReduce by Google and FaceBook was yet another major innovation from another web giant.

2) **Capacity scheduling:**  The capacity scheduler was first developed by **Yahoo.** The original Yahoo capacity scheduler supported several features similar to the FaceBook fair scheduler, but the greater innovative focus was more upon job queues rather than pools:

a) jobstreams are broken out to jobsteps as tasks;

b) each queue can be allocated a share of resources at start of the process;

c) job tasks can be ranked for resource priorities, however, once the process is started there can be no changes unless the job fails and is restarted.

Together, these 3 concepts pioneered by Google, FaceBook and Yahoo, are generally known as 'Big Data Block Parallelism'. It is also worthy to note that these same algorithms were the subject of research and experiments by the famous MIT student Aaron Swartz, who was the founder of 'Demand Progress' websites in opposition to SOPA/PIPA web content censorship, and was prosecuted for testing his brilliant improvements to the Big Data Hadoop 'Block Parallelism' algorithms of these 3 leading emerging multi-billion dollar companies – after he simply downloaded 4,000 academic test files from MIT research (including the controversial research of Dr. Jon Gruber, the renowned 'architect of Obama-Care') – without ever even reading them, yet used the same 'metadata scan indexing' method as NSA was revealed to use by same methods by infamous system administrator whistle-blower Edward Snowden during same time as Swartz prosecution. This resulted in mysterious death of Swartz, which was officially ruled to be a suicide. Yet many technology industry analysts have observed that Swartz could have 'easily advanced upon the early Big Data Hadoop and MapReduce technology from Open Source to have competed easily with all 3 of the early entrants into the Big Data web optimization super vendor businesses, and significantly diminished their massive market share. We can now never know, but it has been widely reported by technology analysts that research of Swartz as a student at MIT had to do with early comparisons of many methods of 'chunking' massive unstructured data to try to compare and evaluate alternate methods (which have been used since his untimely death by many vendors, including by SAS).

This and related methods include different ways to process and manage very huge unstructured data streams into files that are more manageable as multiple blocks than can be scanned for keyword strings, including redundant copies of blocks as files processed in parallel for 'first or fast' solutions involving 'messaging and marshaling' by metadata files that can send very small status update files to a control program on a local or remote server for action.

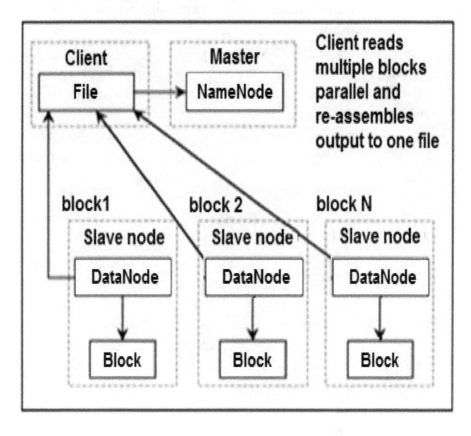

**Figure 4. Big Data Block Parallelism as Expanded by Facebook, Yahoo, and Others for Web Optimization**

++    In all Big Data Hadoop and NoSQL database implementations based on Apache Open Source library specifications, there are at least two supported network architecture partitions as was shown in Figure 4:

1)  Random Partitioner (RP) option: Randomly distributes the key-value pairs over the network, which results in good load balancing of parallel processes and data, but needs core paired-key compares.

2)  Order Preserving Partitioner (OPP): Rank by sorts of 'chunk' cluster blocks to order key-value pairs so that similar data are nearby; advantage is fewer nodes, disadvantage is an uneven distribution of key-value pairs, and uneven size of cluster block nodes, which lead to long waits for large nodes to finish.

A Hadoop cluster basically consists of a single namenode plus a cluster of datanodes. Each datanode within a namenode services orthogonal 'blocks' or 'chunks' of data over a namenode network using a standardized block transmission protocol, which typically involves 64 or 128MB blocks of data. The Hadoop Distributed File System conventionally uses TCP/IP sockets for communication. Local host clients usually submit Remote Procedure Calls (RPC's) to communicate with each other.
       The capabilities to use SAS/BASE to program such Big Data MapReduce functions have been previously demonstrated by David Moors at SAS Global Forum 2014 for SASReduce, based on use of SAS macros similar to implementations of original Google elaborations of basic

27

framework for MapReduce clusters. Thus, Hadoop, MapReduce, and other basic functionality can be provided using very simple SAS coding.

In addition, even the most advanced Big Data Hadoop, MapReduce functionality of both Apache Open Source, as well as Big Data Integration of complex processes can be supported by DI Studio to register metadata and deploy jobs incorporate with source code registered as metadata objects as in Figure 5:

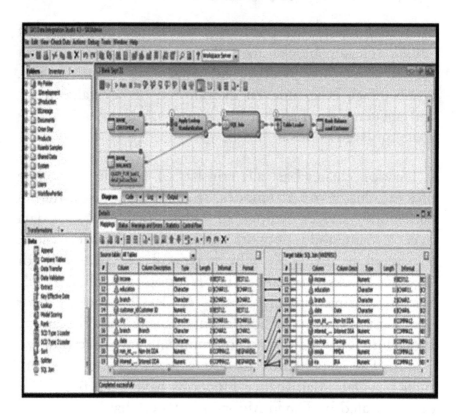

**Figure 5. SAS Data Integration Studio For Metadata Inventory, Transform and Job Process Monitoring**

This includes two very important characteristics that are commonly cited by Big Data purists – which are the fundamental requirements for Replication and Parallelism. These are not easily provided based on SAS Base (or any other language including R or Python libraries from Open Source – and are best provided by either the Apache Open Source project libraries – or major vendor Big Data platform extensions from SAS, IBM and others.

With regard to SASReduce prototypes, this was not provided in the initial version, yet future enhancements to SASReduce may provide this full capability equal to or more than of the leading worldwide IT industry Big Data standalone products – competitive to the free Open Source code libraries from Apache Hadoop, at no low cost of SASReduce for organizations that have SAS, which can be effectively integrated with Apache Hadoop open source (notably SASReduce from SAS Base code is not supported by SAS as user-written macros – similar to Open Source).

Notably all such basic Big Data Hadoop must include the following minimum 2 approaches:

1) <u>Replication</u>: An approach using host node object processes that scan update logs or file size changes to detect data changes, which are copied to temp files until all distributed data files that are in active task processing are updated with the latest changes.

Until all redundant files have been replicated with the same changes, further processing is essentially 'on hold'. This approach is regarded as most reliable; however, it is very time and resource-intensive, so costs more.

29

2) <u>Duplication</u>: An approach which identifies one distributed network database as the master source, then duplicates to several network path locations for parallel processing of multiple tasks, which are then reconciled offline to create a single file or set of data updates to apply to a copy of master source that is output as target ETL data, across operational staging network server locations.

All Hadoop Big Data compliant implementations must also conform to standards for 'NoSQL'. This may be at first confusing; as it really means '**N**ot **ONLY SQL**'. This can also be interpreted as a 'reverse SQL', to only select joins by 'EXCLUDES' rather than 'INCLUDES'.

It supports most SQL syntax conventions, which make it intuitive and easy to learn for SAS Proc SQL programmers; but is even much more extensible, to support more than simple joins.

Notably, these powerful extensions can be implemented to SAS DI Studio project jobs or SAS Stored Processes, and can be implemented within Transform code.

NoSQL is often integrated with other Big Data such as Massive Parallel Distributed Database Processing, as well as Columnar-Based Databases (such as Apache Cassandra – also known as Federated file services), and Database-As-a-Service (DAS, also known as remote co-hosting – or A.K.A. 'The Cloud).

Essentially a DAS 'Cloud' can be managed as a 'Multiple Virtual Systems (MVS) mainframe host network.

The most significant benefits of Hadoop and NoSQL are for applications involving the following:

- <u>Logs</u> and click-stream time-based event recording and journaling with hit count output files

- <u>Web crawling</u> and text archive analysis of unstructured or semi-structured 'corpora' data files

- <u>Searches and scans</u> for keywords or phrases similar to text mining using word-spotting files

One of the most important benefits of Hadoop is that it can link directly with any file system that can be mounted remotely by using a URL web address.

Traditionally, this has usually come at a price – a rise in bandwidth response time due to loss of server locality – and complex downstream accumulated delays even with multi-threaded processes.

However, this is the major benefit of Hadoop and MapReduce clustering when used with remote Cloud services – whereby rather than the high bandwidth needed to move and process large files to internal servers and warehouse data stores – as bulk of historical and high volume data is loaded by DI Studio and accumulated in Cloud servers as off-prime processes, with small message files or updates with new transformations as in Figure 6:

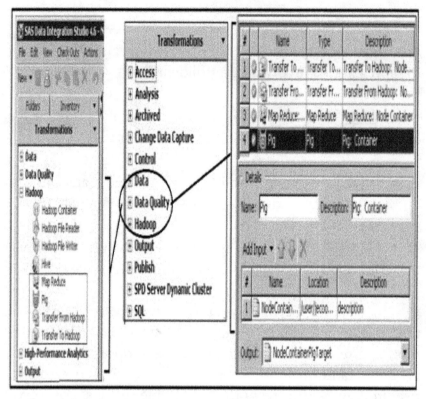

**Figure 6. SAS DI Studio Hadoop Data Transforms
Using Hive, MapReduce and Pig Latin**

Many aspects of Big Data Hadoop and MapReduce have similarities to legacy mainframe and distributed client-server network technology, and are especially relevant to Small Data and Little Data like Android or Arduino.

To reduce network traffic, Hadoop needs to know which servers are closest to the data; as this is the essential strategy that MapReduce must specify as a multi-tiered Cluster Definition and Access Plan.

Such Cluster Definitions within MapReduce are critical to Hadoop and Big Data.

Notably, SAS DI Studio and the Transformations it supports for Hadoop and MapReduce processes provide many advantages.

All of these Big Data Hadoop and Cloud Services can be managed more effectively for Analytics projects and process Data Integration using SAS DI Studio for ETL and ELT processes that can leverage SAS/BASE, SAS/STAT, and other powerful Analytics products such as SAS/OR, SAS/QC, SAS/ETS, SAS/EM, as well as powerful Data Science and Data Management tools such as SAS Management Console and DataFlux Data Quality Management.

Although these Big Data Hadoop products and services are particularly useful to large businesses and organizations, these Big Data Cloud vendors also increasingly offer support for small to midsize distributed Hadoop federated file services, which can also be supported by BASE SASReduce and SAS Macros for Parallel Processing on Bigger or Smaller data load scales.

# CHAPTER 3

## SMALL DATA AND MAP REDUCE FEDERATED FILE SERVER CONCEPTS

Small Data is a term that emerged more recently within the past several years as a top new IT technology buzzword. There are basically two contexts for this term that are related, and both supported by SAS:

1) <u>Small Data as a concept related to use of individual human user responses to both data format and visualization performance metric of effectiveness of social media and web page presentation</u> (such as time-to-consider and pass-through metrics), as has been studied more than two decades by various academic organizations, including MIT Media Lab and Oklahoma State Univ. using SAS; and

2) <u>Small Data using Big Data parallel platforms like Apache Cassandra, advanced by **Twitter**</u> as a way to automate ETL of massive data files based on Hadoop and HDFS with merge joins to multiple disparate small file and tables.

This allows for more flexible architectures which can be designed to optimize network traffic to local sources using SAS with Hadoop Open Source, and even to integrate remote cloud sources with limited data table refresh time – commonly called Federation Server processes – and supported by SAS by DI Studio integration services using new DataFlux Federation Server as in Fig. 7.

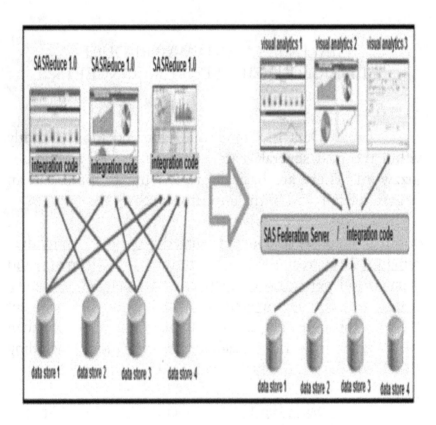

**Figure 7. SAS DataFlux Federation Server for Data Management of Big to Small Data Visual Analytics**

The first of these two major Small Data concepts relates to the integration and optimization of machine learning and artificial intelligence. This involves interesting new niches within Data Science that are essentially side space user domains, such as intelligent mobile phone geo-positional messaging and marketing apps, wearable body attached Personal Area Networks (PAN's) and more, which have long been the focus of research at MIT Media Labs, as well as AT&T Labs among others.

The second concept has been an essential focus of SAS data management and analytics for over two decades. This has included central to distributed SAS network database optimization, based upon both Big Data concepts, as well as this Small Data architecture, now commonly known as Federated servers.

A Federated Server is a Big to Small Data concept, known as a 'Virtual Server'. The main goal of SAS Federated Server, is to store table attribute maps in master server locations – in other words – metadata. SAS was an early pioneer in automated and custom metadata for BI, and DI Studio/DataFlux expands it.

Federated services integrate disparate databases via a flexible centralized platform such as SAS DI Studio to register and link using metadata offers several benefits:

First, federated databases offer an efficient alternative to merging databases together, which can be a tedious labor intensive and risky task.

Second, they help programmers avoid tight coupling of applications using legacy databases by eliminating vendor and legacy database schema lock-in, with cost and time benefits to the enterprise.

The origins of Small Data within the Big Data framework were first pioneered by the Apache Open Source Project Cassandra, which was among the first NoSQL database to prototype Federation file services.

Cassandra was improved upon by SAS in DI Studio DataFlux Federation Server to increase the effectiveness of Hadoop data stores and MapReduce clusters by use of 'dynamic column updates' to achieve data integration and data reduction using virtual partitioning of row groupings.

Rows are organized as tables, and sub-tables or views, which are commonly known as Dimensions, as part of the normal transition as types that can be effectively grouped for optimization as Star Schemas.

The other component of Star Schemas, are organized as Columns into tables known as Facts, which are recalculated as different summarization levels of Dimension averages and sums, versus total Dimensions.

SAS has developed its own approach to Big Data to Small Data Integration, based upon SAS DI Studio and DataFlux Quality Data Management with Federation Server to register and dynamically enhance metadata in a more adaptive and effective manner than other platforms.

Basically, SAS DI Studio has the power not only to reliably standardize and automate ETL and ELT processes – but also has unparalleled capabilities to implement SAS models to create XML and PMML for transformations.

These can include a variety of such transforms, including from simple ETL extract and load processes, as well as complex transforms that include fitting data to a variety of statistical distributions, as well as imputations, as shown in Figure 8:

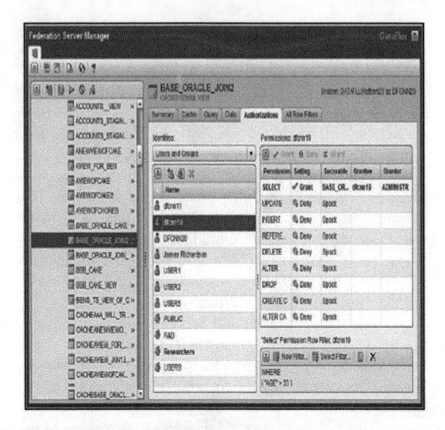

**Figure 8. Hadoop MapReduce Small Data Integration Management Using SAS DataFlux Federation Server**

The benefits of SAS Data Studio and Dataflux Federation Server are for applications that involve:

- <u>Machine learning and artificial intelligence</u> for web-scale to individual response processes

- <u>Real-time data node cluster segmentation</u> and processing of digital imagery and social media

- <u>Dynamic keyword semantic rank analysis</u> and pattern recognition for text standardizations

Notably, SAS Federation Server approaches the dynamics of new emerging data patterns and structures by concurrent offline batch analysis by Hadoop process coding objects to compare to de-normalized tables.

This approach is very resource intensive even as offline or off-prime schedule process to use keywords. This demands costly system resources compared to basic replication and duplication redundancy metrics.

Each component Federated data store or ancillary file system within Hadoop system architectures must be completely self-sustained and functional.

When a SAS Federated Server Metadata-Registered application queries a database, the metadata must determine which of its component databases contains the critical data being requested and automatically passes requests to it.

This involves universal data model mappings of not only the location of a server and file system path as a database connection schema, but also transformations, filters, and quality checks of data. In the case of SAS, the Enterprise BI platform with DI Studio and Quality Data Management with DataFlux Federation Server are a powerful option.

Within the domain of Small Data and Federation file services are even more extremely important concepts to optimize of the Big Data Hadoop to Small Data transformations, the two most important of which are:

- <u>Change Data Capture (CDC)</u> Load Transformations for dynamic edits to map or remap input data

- <u>Slowly Changing Dimensions (SCD)</u> – Type 1 and Type 2 Load Transformations

These Big Data to Small Data Transformation types are supported in SAS DI Studio and DataFlux, as methods for reliable management of gradual systematic 'delta' monitoring, and discrete modification of continuous changes in both Star Schema Dimensions and Fact values that indicate need for stratification. Some of the major benefits of Big Data techniques that can be enhanced by Small Data integration which can be implemented using DI Studio and DataFlux Federation Server (as well as the Big Data Hadoop and MapReduce capabilities supported in SAS/BASE using SASReduce 1.0 for Small Data) include:

- <u>Most businesses and organizations, both large and small, process huge volumes of data</u> from multiple diverse input sources, and the impact on technical labor productivity is enormous.

- <u>Most problems with input data from each external source can be categorized</u> by specific vendor and problem incident types in order to filter and transform future data with programmer managed user defined code objects, and monitored for future ongoing success to prevent similar problems.

- <u>Standardized filters and code edit objects to check and transform data can assure quality</u> and simplify data as well as improve efficiency using SAS Proc Formats and Info Maps, in order to improve performance of cpu and networks by reducing size of lookup tables and transmit files, and users can easily create integrated views of data, as source and target files by versioning.

Data Federation is thus a very powerful method to link Big Data Hadoop to Smaller Data using Data Federation Services in order to link to multiple intranet as internet URL's or websites as well as both Cloud and local host servers, for both large businesses or organizations, as well as small to mid-size businesses across diverse locations in order to optimize management of data across cloud, web and even Local Area Networks.

This includes SAS DI Studio support to most major data vendors, including SAP, Sybase, IBM, Oracle, Teradata, HP Vertica, as well as Microsoft ODBC – and External Flat Files.

SAS DI Studio and Federation Server can link directly to SAS/LASR analytic server, which can also leverage Hadoop and MapReduce for Federation file management of analytic model parameter input and output data objects.

The LASR server has its own HADOOP file storage format, called SAS HDAT, which is highly optimized for fast load of HADOOP data. SAS can also write data in this format from any SAS system using new SAS/ACCESS to load to SAS/LASR.

Data Federation Server is thus a data integration solution that uses metadata linkages to preserve and maintain data integrity.

This differs from traditional ETL and ELT methods because it pulls only the data needed out of source data file systems registered to SAS/DI Studio.

Data Federation is thus Small Data that is ideally suited when working with Big Data because it allows you to work with data stored directly in the source systems.

Using Data Federation you only pull the subset of data that you need when you need it.

Using the SAS Federation Server, you can combine data from multiple sources, manage sensitive data through security features, and improve performance through in-database optimizations when critical data is highly dynamic.

This is also important to management of Little Data Integration with very small messaging and embedded microprocessor log exception file updates as are required for many remote Arduino apps.

# CHAPTER 4

## LITTLE DATA AUTOMATION FOR ANDROID OR ARDUINO TO HADOOP INTEGRATION

Little Data is an even more recent term related to potential to integrate advanced analytics into Big Data to enhance current Data Science, by leveraging advanced statistical platforms such as provided by SAS.

The distinction between Small Data and Little Data can be understood in the comparison between Cloud based **Twitter** and **Arduino** (or **Android** programming apps)

Within the Big Data domain, Twitter and other Small Data involve Federated file systems that can be optimized as data blocks or message packets.

They can be indexed and joined by some type of intelligent primary key structure for dynamic sorting of parallel segments.

The Twitter 'hash-tag' prefix is a unique primary key for sorting '**#xxx**' messages for distribution to millions of user nodes per second.

Twitter first approached Little Data in offline counting of hash-tags for realtime 'trending ranks', and since then social media users desire increasingly complex offline processes easily satisfied by SAS Analytics.

**Android** and **Arduino** are arguably the most flexible programmable microprocessor platforms for Big to Little Data  applications (and to a slightly lesser extent, Android related platforms) for realtime parallel interfaces – both directly, and indirectly to Cloud services – as well as 'middle-tier' servers (or scalable desktops and laptops), which are most relevant here for local host 'visual analytics' apps, such as from SAS or Cloud, shown in Figure 9:

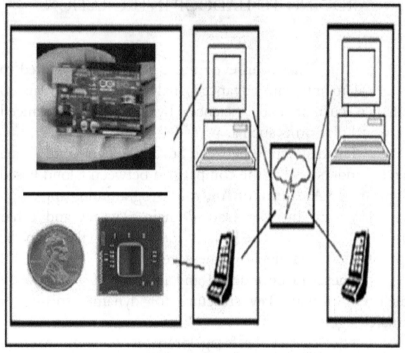

**Figure 9. Typical Little Data Microprocessor Linkages to Cloud via Local and Remote Hosts**

In the previous figure, both Android and Arduino microprocessors are shown graphically for their potential each to link to either a local host PC computer (including laptops) and/or to a local Personal Area Network (PAN) software application with direct linkage to remote host computer or computers (including across the Cloud).

Thus, it is possible to support Little Data apps for software based ETL and statistical imputation of data gaps as well as automated correction of transmission interrupts and corrupted data errors or exceptions that can be edited using multiple imputation techniques supported by SAS, or R, Python and other Open Source statistical libraries (or other Little Data platforms from IBM, SAP and others).

This includes both advanced SAS analytics techniques to develop algorithms and models that can be incorporated (or even efficiently hardcoded, as in the case of EEPROM's in microprocessor devices such as Arduino) – or incorporated into remote to host data messaging algorithms for smart phone apps for local or remote hosts including Cloud hosting.

This includes two major benefits of advanced analytics as provided by SAS platforms and products for Data gap imputation; and Linear model projections – thus:

1) Little Data is not only Small, as multiple disparate data sources often need to be integrated by joins at time of ETL to targets for Big Data files and tables – but is aptly also characterized as <u>Little Data with high proportions of missing, interrupted transmissions, or other suspense data gaps</u> – which may require many transformation passes of source data input to convert to multiple imputation files

that can be archived for offline manual and automated analysis code, as appropriate using SAS/DI/DataFlux; and

2) <u>Little Data is usually implemented to segment data from large Big Data stores</u>, using class mapping tables to prepare for Small Data groupings or individual account lookups – as demonstrated here for simple Arduino subject attached devices as controlled by SAS DI Studio and DataFlux

As for the Little Data architecture hardware and microprocessor system platforms to accommodate such data acquisition inputs to Big Data on local host computers or across the Cloud.

As shown in the previous figure, there are many micro-system architectures and footprints (or much more appropriately 'thumbprints' (or 'toe-prints') that can provide for both of two Little Data alternatives to collect and store to send data streams for Big Data processing.

The first microprocessor architecture is from all of the super-small 'micro' processors that were developed first for use in hand-held mobile cell phones, such as the Intel Atom, which was miniaturized down to less than 1x1 inch (roughly the size of a US penny coin). This architecture has had many embodiments, including smart phones such as Blackberry, Raspberry Pi, and **Android**, among others.

The second and more recent microprocessor architecture involves a series of 'mini'-system processors that are more often referred to by 'handprint' size more in the range to fit in a 'pocket' in wearable human applications for Personal Area Network (PAN) system nodes, and more commonly about 2x3 inches (roughly the size of a deck of playing cards. This architecture also has several system embodiments, but the early leader in this class has been the **Arduino** microprocessor series from Italy Turin Open Source project (which since it was introduced has already after less than a decade to has inspired several clones).

Both **Android** and **Arduino** were first developed and supported as Open Source projects, same as the Apache Open Source Big Data projects, and are together foundations for two alternative Little Data architecture platforms – as each involve embedded processors that can be programmed with software for intelligent data acquisition to pre-process inputs to impute data gaps or map using core lookup tables based on ranges or keywords.

Just as with Big Data Open Source beginning with the Apache Open Source Big Data Hadoop and Small Data MapReduce projects, the original Apache worldwide Open Source projects were advanced under the Open Source licenses (which basically involves to certify start point from 'frozen' code from the original Open Source public domain version, then the right for individuals or companies to modify with comments as new independent release that they can maintain or not based on the type of Open Source license they choose to publish – including to offer as either a new Open Source project, or to offer as a commercial product that can even be patented (such as was the case with the early innovations to Big Data Hadoop and Small Data MapReduce by Facebook, Google, Yahoo, Twitter, Amazon, Microsoft and many others.

In this case, with Android and Arduino, there were also early innovations, mostly from academic institutions, which were part of original Apache Open Source projects, and then later became Little Data foundations that were in the case of Android advanced by many of the same companies that were instrumental to the previous Big Data and Small Data innovations and enhancements.

In the case of Android Little Data, many individual academics contributors, the U.S. government, as well as several major corporations were to major supporters to extend the base code from Apache Android project. One of the most significant was Google, who led in the development of Android Eclipse IDE, shown in Figure 10.

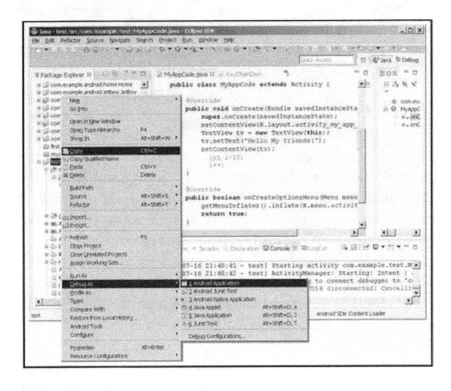

**Figure 10. Android Eclipse IDE to Manage Java Open Source Samples and Debug-Test Code Changes**

The Android Eclipse IDE and SDK supported by Google and others for extensions for the programming of chips such as Intel Atom series were used in many very successful smart cell phones produced by such major companies as Samsung, LG, Erickson and more.

This has included extension of the Android IDE for Eclipse (which was basically a Java IDE for basic Apache Android), to more GUI based Java extensions to include a 'remote control' style app for virtual simulation and testing of the Java code from Eclipse as in Figure 11.

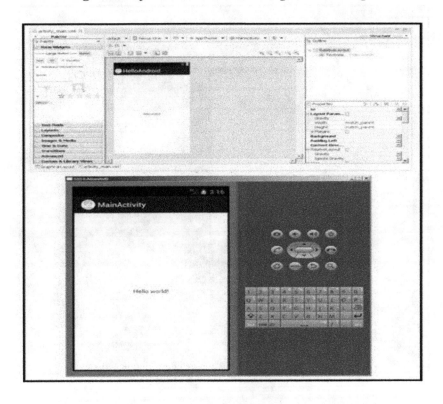

**Figure 11. Android Google Recommended Eclipse Main Activity Display with Default from Google API**

As of 2015 (when the First Edition of this book was published) the software for Android Eclipse as supported by Google and their partners have been extended to support smart phones and clones more similar to the Apple iPad, again with help from smart phone hardware vendors such as Samsung, LG and Erickson.

As shown n Figure 12, a default screen display for the most recent Android IDE is the Google search screen (as a new proprietary version of traditional 'Hello World'.)

**Figure 12. Android SDK and IDE to Manage Code and Test with Google Recommended Eclipse**

The Google supported Eclipse IDE and SDK in Open Source and in the API available for iPad-clone smart phone app developers using their Google Cloud services are also similar to many of the other leading Cloud services from Amazon, Microsoft as well as smaller emerging mid-size Cloud services.

This also includes several emerging smart phone app development architecture platforms for Little Data programming for hand-held applications, including for the marshalling and control or monitoring of communications from a smart phone such as Android (or other embedded slave processors including Arduino cluster node sensors).

This includes several 'small footprint' software platforms for development of mobile device software from IBM, SAP, Oracle and others; and SAS Visual Analytics

For most SAS Visual Analytics applications that can be integrated into Intranet and Cloud services using SAS DI Studio, a smart phone platform such as Android has preceded the new opportunity for both Android and Arduino related embedded programming microprocessors.

Yet, Arduino provides a wider range of new application possibilities – as a new 'hands-free automation' technology that can extend a hand-held smart phone or local host laptop or desktop PC with a wide variety of sensor types that can be networked as slaves to master nodes, which can be programmed as Hadoop and MapReduce clusters with SAS pre-processing.

Although the true official Arduino boards are manufactured only in Italy, the Arduino base 'mother' board was cleverly designed to handle most common categories of sensors and stacked 'shield' boards as simple plug-ins (all categories of which are provided for in both hardware and software IDE of Arduino). Arduino software control coding objects are known as "sketches".

Arduino UNO board and IDE is most popular, and comes with hundreds of examples as in Figure 13:

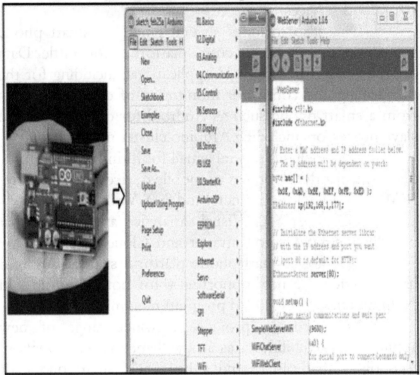

**Figure 13. Little Data from Arduino UNO Embedded Microprocessor Board to Arduino Sketches Code IDE**

From the beginning of the project in Italy at Turin Interaction Design Institute, the culture and concept of the Arduino was intended as a new model of computer app development similar to the long tradition of Italian art work projects as a craft by teams of artisans.

These sketches are thus based upon the transition of apprentices to master status based on contributions to libraries of programming object code.

Within the past decade, the library of Arduino sketches has increased to several dozen categories, each with several dozen public domain 'best practice' open source code objects, for a total of many hundreds of C code object programs – notably similar and to origins of Apache Hadoop Open Source as expanded by its many supporters.

As originally conceived, default basic language for all Arduino sketch code objects is native C. Each app category and 'Best Practices' code type accepted to publish in each release of the Arduino IDE must be coded with comments in simple C language, and header include libraries must be coded in C++, with certification of all extensible drivers, internal table mappings, and default variable parameter attributes.

The Arduino UNO was designed to fit in the palm of a human hand, and is slightly smaller than a 'deck of playing cards'.

It can be powered by a 'digital watch battery', or charged via a USB cable, as well as options for stackable 'independent power enabled sensor 'shields'.

The base Arduino UNO board has a dedicated logic processor, and both a USB and Serial connector for physical linkages to sensors for input and output or communication linkages to slave or master node devices.

Dedicated data storage is supported by removable SD drive cards or by USB flash drives.

Master data acquisition control programs can be 'virtually burned' as EEPROM's for a multitude of functions to configure each Arduino as either a master or slave device.

Normally, up to 3 simple 'single wire' sensors (or a single 'three wire' sensor; or two sensors for 'one' plus 'two' wire) are supported on a single board – and then shields can be stacked with usually same number of sensor inputs to a specialized embedded logic microprocessor.

Depending on the 'stack footprint' of the shield, up to 3 or 4 shields can be stacked up to one inch thick.

Although some applications can be served by 'standalone' embedded Arduino board storage, by far the most common and extensible configurations involve the use of Radio Frequency (RF), Infrared (IR) or Wireless Ethernet (WIFI) linkages to cell phones, internet or intranet servers, or even Cloud servers.

Notably, the Arduino can be configured as a 'micro ISP web server' to send emails, or as a 'virtual cell phone' to send text messages or pre-recorded voice messages, as well as log data streams to hosts.

Notably, a 'shield' is basically an add-on that is activated by 'plug-ons' on top of the Arduino UNO that conform to specifications of such hardware and is certified by Arduino in Italy.

In some cases, there are simple 'wire insertion clamps' and in others there must be soldering in order to link the Arduino UNO (which is essentially a super-miniaturized motherboard) to the stacks of specialized application shields that are 'plugged-in' on top of it.

Depending on the application needs as a trade-off of how many sensor and communication types are required, it may be possible to stack many layers of shields onto a single Arduino UNO – or else it may be better to stack only one shield layer each onto two Arduino UNO boards – which can be integrated with similar Master-Slave configurations as Hadoop for Big Data.

For most software programmers and analysts, the hardware considerations can be very intimidating (to say the least); and for SAS programmers or software engineers who do not have background experience in electronics, this can be daunting, especially the need for soldering.

However, many are curious and would like to try Arduino. Stacked boards include 'wire pin clip options', as well both 'pre-soldered' and hybrid 'pre-soldered and wire pin clip boards' for building modular prototypes

This is also a major innovation from Arduino project movement, as the Arduino UNO base 'baby mama' microprocessor mother board anticipated the need to expand to handle up to dozens of individual sensors, and allow for future sensor combinations for emerging application domains as 'stackables'.

These shield boards can provide support for fast prototyping of embedded sensor processor apps grouped by category IDE templates.

In addition to Arduino shields, which can be 'stacked' using standard processor board linkage bus pin alignments, there are also multiple pin positions for sensors – which include single-wire, two-wire interface (TWI) or interface squared communication (I2C), as well as 3-wire sensors and arrays – and Serial Peripheral Interface (SPI) and Serial UAT with Transistor Translator Logic (TTL).

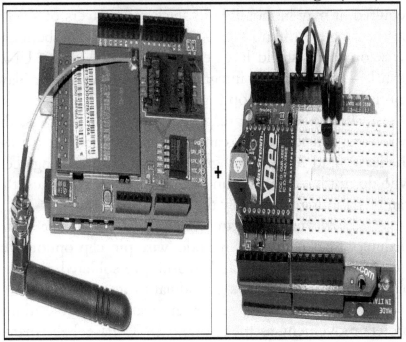

**Figure 14. Arduino UNO Board with RF and Ethernet Wireless Stacker Shields for GPS Data Integration**

Complex pin settings and soldering skills for traditional electronics can quickly cause damage from one mistake; but Arduino makes soldering virtually obsolete – for more programming with less electronics. Thus, many Arduino expansion vendors around the world offer Arduino 'turn-key' kits over the internet with specialized shields and sensors pre-soldered, tested and 'RF/WIFI ready', as shown in Figure 14.

These methods involve direct wired connections between multiple Arduino boards and standalone sensors, using hardwired harnesses, for human wearable Personal Area Networks (PANs), like micro-LANS also attachable to animals, robots, or vehicles. Each Arduino board can also have a variety of local fixed storage devices, including USB flash drives or Secure Digital (SD) memory cards used in smart phones and digital cameras – the main disadvantage of which is that 2 to even 32 GB drives can fill up quickly even with very short log formats at moderate sample rates. Thus, remote linkages such as RF or WIFI wireless, are preferred, despite they are a bit expensive; but the convenience for more flexible automation is well worth it. Also, SD memory cards are supported by all basic Arduino boards including the UNO, and are advisable as a good option for physical local backup recovery of all local resident data if needed.

Yet after almost a decade of 'official' Arduino boards produced in Italy, and Arduino-compatible shields mostly produced from China – within the last year a new second of generation 'Arduino clones' have been also introduced from US and UK among other nations – which provide a 'smaller subset of basic Arduino capabilities' (usually USB, Ethernet and EEPROM as a start) – but with a much smaller 'thumbprint' – Arduino 'clones' are often 'size of a postage stamp vs deck of cards' – as 1x1 inch (even down to thumbprints of .5x.5 inch single sensor shields – with USB to smart phone or web servers).

Many of these new Arduino clone boards and 'micro-shields' were crowd-funded on KickStarter.com, which includes many sensor shields (as well as even digital cameras)', which not only fit on top of the new 'Arduino micro clone board' standards. This includes Kick Starter project for 'Easy Plug Cam' (which includes digital cameras with very small footprints – which were prototyped for 'wearable law enforcement digital video cameras', after many incidents involving controversial events which could have been resolved by automated and independent archival of wearable cam controllers) as shown in Figure 15:

**Figure 15. Arduino Next Generation 'Clone Boards' for 'Mini to Micro Shields' To Downsize Little Data Apps**

The critical importance of this most recent generation of 'Arduino clones' should be easily understood, as it is as equally as significant as the 'PC clone' revolution that occurred over two decades ago – which was to result in several rapid new generations of personal computing hardware and applications. In this case the most significant long term implications are not so much the reduction of size – but the fact that instead of a single 'card deck sized' Arduino microprocessor can provide standardized shield sensor management services – as 'micro-Arduino' slave nodes linked to a master Arduino 'micro-web server' for the management of data as a down-scaled version of a 'Local Area Network' PC server.

This should be easily understood as new platform to develop 'wearable Personal Area Network (PAN)' apps as first envisioned by MIT Media Lab – and likely to become a critical new generation technology. This is a newly emerging technology advancement opportunity that will likely be on the cutting edge over the next decade.

Yet notably, the critical path of future applications of this technology should be clear. Although simple 'one-up' prototypes are fairly easy for hobbyists and projects such as on Kick Starter, it is much more difficult to scale-up basic PAN applications for thousands (let alone millions) of accounts with protocols and standards that support parallel intelligent processing for near-realtime reliable response. However, there is already precedence of technology – in cell phone telecommunications – that is also related – and by hybridizing both Arduino with Android together in PAN applications provides even greater opportunities.

# CHAPTER 5

## PROTOTYPE APPS OF LITTLE DATA ANDROID AND ARDUINO TO HADOOP BIG DATA CONCEPTS

Basically, applications of this technology to support scalable large scale business operations is similar to development of cellular mobile phone industry – however, this new emerging 'Personal Area Network' technology involves not only the operations research optimizations for efficiency of bandwidth and throughput of realtime audio – but also the new wrinkle of new benefits to summarize data by ranges and categories automated in EEPROM's, as optimized by offline Advanced Analytics such as SAS, and with data integration such as DI Studio and data management such as DataFlux Federation Server.

Although the technical specification and configuration of terminal and network node communications may be somewhat more within the common comfort level range of SAS Platform Administrators and Server Admins for most common operating systems, this may also be daunting for SAS users.

63

Yet these are well within the range of tasks that most SAS Architects and Admins can easily support – since the Arduino microprocessor boards are actually very similar but simpler than much more powerful desktops and laptops that are installed with SAS software.

In effect, the Arduino microprocessor board and other Little Data apps – including smart cell phone apps using Android, Bluetooth or Apple – as well as Cloud based web-crawler programs including Twitter trending agents – are all essentially slaves or slave agents that provide new data updates to hosts or 'overseer' slaves, which pre-process Arduino and other Small Data packets to host networks with SAS software that can be used to 'clean' and impute the raw data.

This need for platform architecture and services to support Small and Little Data within Big Data Hadoop has already been anticipated by several leading Cloud service vendors, including Google and Amazon.

Following is shown a Google-recommended Open Source remote terminal device communications app that can be used to configure an Arduino board with RF or WIFI shields and Real Time Clock (RTC) as well as GPS sensors to output a standard time-based 'difference' log to either 'onboard flash drive' and/or RF or WIFI transmission to nearby local host PC or laptop with web connectivity to Cloud server – as in Figure 16:

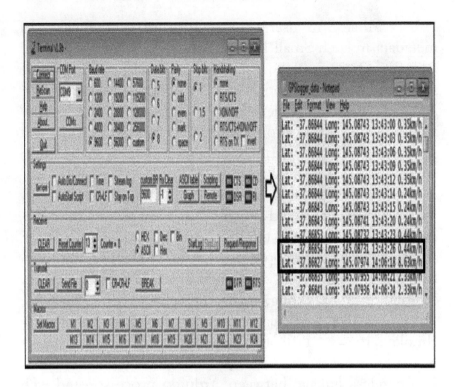

**Figure 16. Arduino Compatible Telecommunications Console Logging of GPS Time-Based Series Data**

Notably, this Google Open Source API is a simple version of the same or similar technology that has been often highlighted in TV and movies related to official law enforcement and government as well as others to monitor a vehicle by attachment of a wireless GPS device to track persons of interest.

Google pioneered this technology to transmit and store on Cloud servers as metadata for future analysis, and was advanced extensively by US government DHS and other agencies for protection and security.

Most SAS users are well aware of the value of metadata in such Small Data inputs and updates for Cloud and Big Data processing to build, recalibrate and refine statistical predictive models and segment profiles.

Thus the simple GPS 'Lat/Long' with 'Time-base' at any change in location and/or acceleration rate is most significant, as this is normally similar to data series that SAS analysts are accustomed to work with.

Many Arduino sensor types are supported by design and available add-ons include, but are not limited to, shields for:   angles, temperature, humidity barometer, accelerometer, gyroscopic angle, servo stepper, infrared, RF, WIFI, USB,  flash drive, and even turnkey boards for cell phone robot texting, email and web servers.

In this particular example, the log is 'time-base chunked' to a '*.txt' file that reflects:

1) a wireless linkage between Arduino processor and web page registered with Google Cloud services; and

2) asynchronous wireless updates to GPS log streams with simple GPS coordinates, time stamps, and acceleration rates which are updated as messages sent from Arduino only if different location and/or acceleration rate.

For purposes to expand beyond this single example to automate and segment by individual account, customer, patient, or groups of similar demographics or segmentation profiles, it is necessary to input this data to a Statistical Analytics platform such as SAS – which can also benefit from DI Studio and DataFlux.

In October of 2014, there were growing concerns among the American people, and the entire world, related to numerous incidents of Ebola infection exposures that involved voluntary monitoring of body temperatures twice daily, and voluntary commitments to limit personal travel using public transportation.

In several cases, there were casual violations of these commitments which caused public concerns to a level approaching panic.

Fortunately, these concerns turned out in retrospect to be over reactions.

Yet, in a stark pragmatic analysis, it can be argued that this should be a 'wake up' call – to prepare for future mass pandemic incidents that may involve actual endangerment of wide populations due to such actions.

To this day, the primary method to screen international airline passengers is a fast body temperature reading as they pass through security to board airlines.

Yet, using this outbreak as an example, subjects may not exhibit any symptoms including elevated temperatures for up to a week, but can still infect others for up to 3 weeks.

This made it critical to come up with either full quarantine strategies, or else to ask potentially exposed individuals entering the United States to voluntarily agree to wear such intelligent monitoring devices of body temperature and GPS location history in order to avoid full quarantines.

This was thus the basis for scenarios that were proposed to expand from the Google API for an Arduino project that was first proposed as support for technical evaluation of feasibility of several Kick Starter projects, as well as demonstration prototypes to scale up such individual Arduino as well as Arduino clone small footprint boards for a single user monitoring device and infrastructure using Google Cloud (as well as the Amazon Cloud) – as a Big Data to Small Data platform solution by this author based upon SAS DI Studio and DataFlux to manage remote web services from Arduino across remote web Clouds. An example of this data acquisition using Arduino is shown with 5 minute re-sampling in Figure 17:

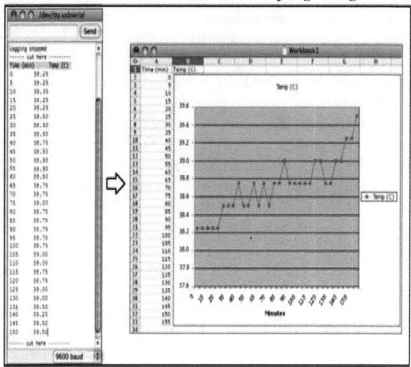

## Figure 17. Arduino Microprocessor Log Real-Time Human Body Temperature Alert Activated Data

*(Where >= 37 C [~ 98.6 F] sets Activation Alert for GPS Monitoring with 5 minute Temperature Sampling)*

In this particular scenario and simulation using SAS/Stats, SAS/OR and SAS/ETS, it was first assumed that one-to-many monitoring of subjects based on 3 real events as prior seeds of a returning potentially deadly infected doctor, nurse and patient were to enter U.S. without mandatory quarantine and were only subject to voluntary monitoring of body temps twice daily.

Even as their body temperatures rose above normal levels (yet likely also impacted their best judgment), each moved freely among major populations. Despite that in such cases, worse scenarios did not occur – this event should be a 'wake up call' to warn of potential dangers from future epidemic events. These scenarios were used for SAS based simulation and analysis of such risks, as well as to evaluate feasibility and potential benefits for continued research and development of body-attached wearable Arduino microprocessors to combine GPS, body temperature, and real-time clock with WIFI wireless shields to transmit regular updates of temps and location if activated as above normal body temperature.

Notably, in this Kick-Starter project, the additional benefits of technology of both Big Data segmentation to individual Ss or patients for multiple monitoring using Google and Amazon Cloud services, are critical; as well as use of SAS Federated Server file administration to leverage realtime SAS Analytics via DI Studio (as well as Visual Analytics technology, and SAS/BASE such as SASReduce).

As shown in the previous figure, as an alternative between full quarantine and voluntarily 'honor system' self-monitoring of subjects returning from regions with risk of outbreak exposures, the Arduino based wearable body temp location monitor is assigned for direct body surface ambulatory attachment. The device is locally programmed to 'awake' every 5 minutes and take a body temperature sample. If the body temperature is normal, the device 'sleeps' for 5 minutes until it takes another data sample. But if the body temperature is elevated more than 1 degree C., and/or if accelerometer and GPS differences indicate rapid changes in subject location, a signal message is sent to a remote host to notify multiple remote Cloud programs to begin accepting temperature and GPS coordinates – as well as send text and email messages to notify public health officials, and archive 10 second samples to a flash drive.

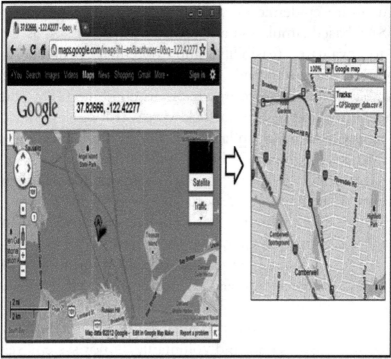

**Figure 18. Google Cloud API Based Real-Time Monitor Geo-Mapping Visualization of GPS Data**

Thus, time-based GPS positions as well as temperature are possible to log minute-by-minute as well as map subject mobility during the time frame when their body temperatures are first elevated to be effectively analyzed by health officials to help identify possible cross exposure, as are shown in Figure 18:

This particular simulation was developed for 1000 runs using SAS MCMC (Monte Carlo Markov Chains), based upon original data in CDC and WHO studies that use SAS/STAT and SAS/OR for such analysis.

In this case, the original source data were compiled based upon multiple data inputs including cell phone records that were to include GPS positions, supplemented by local transportation including Uber taxi positional tracking and subject smart phone GPS data, along with subject body-attached Arduino microprocessor board with temperature sensor, accelerometer, Real Time Clock, GPS and WIFI shields for transmission of log data streams to a Cloud web server, and flash drive for local storage backup.

Obviously, this Arduino demonstrated simulation to leverage Cloud services and API from Google can be a powerful introduction to basic technology of each.

Yet, the reality is that in order to be truly useful, this Kick Starter project would need to be rapidly scalable for thousands of simultaneous users parallel monitoring subjects to dynamically target the handful that demonstrated risk symptoms in October 2014 severe enough to elevate monitoring and trigger back tracking of possible exposures.

Although only a few people died from these events, the costs to contain and protect the general public were many Millions of $US dollars (and could have been Billions – or could even have led to a world pandemic); therefore, we should all regard these past events as a 'learning experience' and 'warning' in order to better prepare for such potential future health care emergencies with technology and best practices such as can be provided by more advanced unobtrusive 'voluntary personal monitoring' technology such as Arduino.

It should be noted that many such Arduino based prototypes have been developed in the past several years, with a multitude of Arduino prototypes for many single-use applications, they have not yet been the focus of technology for scalability to thousands or even millions of users within subject domains.

Despite this was anticipated by Google, Amazon, Yahoo and others, there are several technical problems:

- <u>Gaps in time-base data due to transmission errors</u> and quality of Little Data initiated messaging

- <u>Need for more dynamic imputations of data gaps</u> to handle changing dimensions of such inputs

With regard to the two unique aspects of Little Data – including the need for imputation of asynchronous data points in time series and/or location path series data, and the need for implementing conditional status data splitting and data edit business rule logic – both are easier to implement from Arduino data inputs as statistically optimized data packets or data streams using SAS DI Studio and DataFlux on SAS Federation Server which is configured for inputs from multiple Arduino microprocessor devices – including WIFI and 'micro' web server linkages to local or remote hosts, as well as Big Data Cloud services – which has additional advantage of near-realtime data registration, translation and sort-merge to Hadoop tables, which can be managed to process Arduino log data transmitted to a local host desktop or laptop (or intelligent WIFI relay device) stored process linkage to Cloud services by DI Studio as in Figure 19:

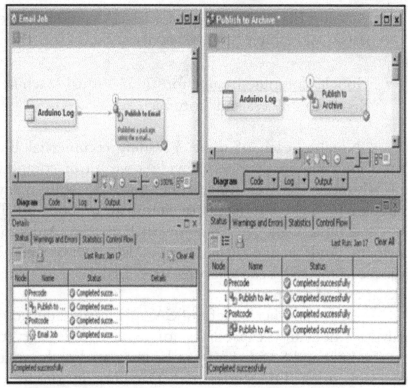

**Figure 19.  SAS DI Studio User Defined Transforms and Job Links to Cloud for Emails and Archival**

There are 3 comprehensive and seminal Big Data Remote Cloud service providers that are most often recommended by leading IT industry studies by Gartner, Forrester and McKinsey, who have been among the forefront of Hadoop and MapReduce related technology, and support most desired architectures:

- <u>Microsoft Azure</u> Hadoop Cloud Services for Big and Little Data with Hortonworks

- <u>Amazon Elastic</u> MapReduce, Elastic Compute Cloud (EC2) and Simple Storage Service (S3)

- <u>Google Compute Engine</u> for Cloud Virtual Machine Rental to Process and Store Big Data

Notably, each of these 3 leading commercial Big Data Cloud remote services provide a wealth of complex and advanced API example code libraries (with many examples to build interfaces for automate of both Small Data and Little Data gap processes such as SAS, Arduino, its clones, Android and many others). Also, each of these 3 major commercial vendors offer free trial accounts (via links at end of this paper).

As yet another benefit of SAS platforms, advanced analytics modeling capabilities of SAS LASR server, SAS/EMiner and SAS/STAT can be integrated as dynamic processes using DI Studio and DataFlux in order to develop 'scoring' algorithms that can be burned into 'virtual EEPROM' sketches on Arduino using C++ or Java classes that can optimize Little Data Arduino 'Proc Format' code messaging scalable to Big Data Cloud using Hadoop to support hundreds or even thousands of concurrent users or more, for a wide variety of applications such as 'Virtual Quarantine' monitor in the previous Kick Starter project.

In the Kick Starter projects evaluated using SAS simulations as previously described, the primary focus related to examples for 'virtual remote monitoring' by Arduino microprocessor data of potentially dangerous events in real-time within range of voluntary self-monitoring versus mandatory quarantine, after they accept to wear near real time temperature and location monitor devices upon arrival at major international airports from originations that have high risk of health contagion outbreaks.

Acceptance to wear such Arduino devices might have stopped subjects from violating personal self-monitor rules. Kick Starter and other crowd funding organizations continue to provide fast start-up operations based on many prototypes involving Little Data apps that leverage both Android and Arduino hardware and software extensions from their Open Source origins.

CHAPTER 6


LARGE HADOOP TO SMALL TO LITTLE DATA
AUTOMATION OF ANDROID
OR ARDUINO APPLICATIONS


There are at this time several Big Data Remote Cloud service providers, as well as even a few Small Data Cloud service providers (which is a new trend also first pioneered on Kick Starter to support Hadoop and MapReduce based on Apache Open Source, including Little Data such as Arduino) – which are all adaptable to a the use of SAS DI Studio and DataFlux to manage and automate use of SAS/STAT Procs or other SAS Analytics platform options for complex data gap imputations not available elsewhere.

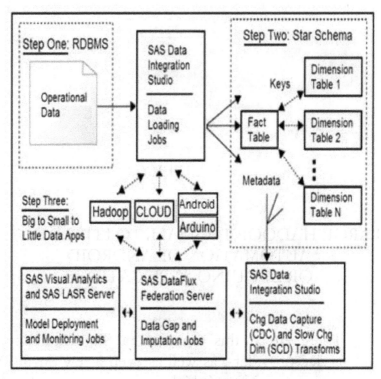

**Figure 20. SAS Based Architecture Platforms to
Support Big Data to Little Data Integrations**

Thus, a highly recommended architecture for most organizations involves to span from traditional RDBMS and operational data warehouses, to Star Schemas, using SAS platforms is shown above in Figure 20.

This solution is based on Data Integration centralized management using SAS DI Studio, with additional automation capabilities if it is configured with SAS DataFlux Federation Server, and with additional extensibility using SAS Analytics LASR Server and SAS Visual Analytics for advanced mobile applications.

SAS DI Studio is a leading solution for Big Data Hadoop and Cloud services, and a prime choice for Big Data Loads and ETL; and SAS DataFlux is a leading solution for Federated file services, and a prime choice for automation of ETL and ELT filters, data gap imputation, and archival of past descriptive statistics to support monitoring model performance and recalibration of coefficients, with unique capabilities when used with SAS Visual Analytics and LASR Server. Arduino data inputs now offer a new potential Little Data layer of potential solutions for both Large to Small organizations using SAS.

As Big Data based on Apache Open Source Hadoop and commercial Cloud Services such as Google to pioneer MapReduce technology matures into its second decade, nearly a decade of parallel maturing of the technology related to Arduino embedded programming microprocessors are now ready for integration using SAS products such as DI Studio, DataFlux Federation Server, LASR Server, and Visual Analytics.

The extensive sensor compatibilities of the base Italian Arduino UNO board standards, and a vast variety of specialized 'turn-key' pre-soldered and 'pin-clipped' Arduino shields from Asian, Euro and US vendors, as well as the new smaller footprint 'Arduino clone' boards that can be networked together as slave nodes to a full Arduino UNO master node – provide capability to design and configure 'Personal Area Networks' (PAN's) as first envisioned by MIT Media Labs and others over twenty years ago.

Yet never before until now was it possible to implement using technology scaled down from traditional

'Local Area Networks' (as well as Big Data Hadoop and MapReduce node clusters), as a new logical and physical 'micro sub-layer'.

Google developed the original extensions of Hadoop for original MapReduce, yet Google no longer uses MapReduce for its own Big Data processing (yet continues to provide it as an option for its Cloud services customers who have complex legacy MapReduce code applications that are too expensive to remediate). Google has developed an entirely new technology that are more similar to the most advanced capabilities of Microsoft Azure and Amazon Elastic Cloud Service Extensions – some of which are now available in free Open Source from Apache as Hadoop 2.0 – which are options for small to mid-size organizations that feel they have abundant hardware and low programmer costs (which may be the only option for many off-shore and particularly Asia companies – yet ultimately more costly and for most US companies).

In the case of Arduino (as well as increasingly complex Android and other smart phone applications), it is no longer normally possible to use simpler traditional Hadoop and MapReduce or even Federation file services, such as are possible for very large scale applications involving massive parallel processing realtime sorts and merges on powerful Cloud servers for simple message applications such as Twitter.

In order to achieve the full potential of Arduino (as well as complex Android and smart phone applications), it is necessary to provide for additional processing layers, in order to provide for capabilities such as:

- <u>Trigger alert messaging</u> based upon threshold or range exceptions (as in the temperature example)

- <u>Initiate log stream</u> archival and data sampling of messages and parameters (as in the GPS example)

- <u>Dynamically score embedded program</u> models to change local parameters for conditional response

Most of the leading IT and Cloud service vendors are attempting to develop such analytics based Big Data Science applications and platforms, using R and Python related Open Source library extensions.

However, few are as extensible and powerful as SAS solutions that span from Big Data to Small, as well as the new Little Data.

Emerging Arduino technology can especially benefit from the uniquely powerful and flexible Analytics and Programming platforms offered by SAS, and the author invites other SAS Analysts and Programmers to participate in the future development of this new emerging technology.

# APPENDIX A:

# APACHE HADOOP & MAPREDUCE EXAMPLES

Apache Open Source Project with contributors from around the world were primary originators of both design and code for Big Data Hadoop and MapReduce. Under the Open Source standard licensing agreements, established commercial vendors and start-up innovators, as highlighted earlier in this book. Following is actual Apache Open Source Project code in XML and Java as examples.

## A1) HADOOP FACEBOOK FAIR SCHEDULER

One of the very first start-ups to leverage the Apache Open Source Project for Big Data was Facebook. The following XML sample was one of the simplest and most elegant solutions to the initial programmer applicant timed tests in the 2010 Oscar-winning movie "The Social Network", about Facebook founder Mark Zuckerberg.

Notably, this code is not fully executable without

additional object code from Apache Big Data libraries, however, it introduces the simple 4 parameters for the earliest Facebook enhancement to Apache Big Data for the "Fair Scheduler" as described earlier in this book: "Minimum Mappings, Minimum Reducers, Maximum Mappings, Maximum Reducers":

```xml
<?xml version="1.0"?>

<!—THIS IS A BASIC FACEBOOK SCHEDULER -->

<allocations>
  <pool name="sample_pool">
    <minMaps>5</minMaps>
    <minReduces>5</minReduces>
    <maxMaps>25</maxMaps>
    <maxReduces>25</maxReduces>

<minSharePreemptionTimeout>300</minSharePree
mptionTimeout>
  </pool>
  <user name="sample_user">
    <maxRunningJobs>6</maxRunningJobs>
  </user>
  <userMaxJobsDefault>3</userMaxJobsDefault>

<fairSharePreemptionTimeout>600</fairSharePr
eemptionTimeout>
</allocations>

<property>
<name>mapred.fairscheduler.poolnameproperty<
/name>
  <value>mapred.job.queue.name</value>
</property>
```

# A2) HADOOP YAHOO CAPACITY SCHEDULER

One of the very first established commercial vendor giants to enhance Apache Open Source Project code libraries for Big Data was Yahoo.  The following XML sample is a much more complex implementation of the Yahoo innovation for a Big Data "Capacity Scheduler". This Yahoo enhancement code is much less dependent on the original Apache Open Source Big Data libraries than the previous Facebook scheduler.  It has been compared to many of the legacy IBM mainframe operating system multiple virtual scheduling foundations advanced by CA and others, updated for web and internetworks for high performance search engines for 'parallel' queue optimizations using Hadoop and MapReduce foundations.

```xml
<?xml version="1.0"?>

<!—THIS IS MORE COMPLEX YAHOO SCHEDULER -->

<configuration>

 <!-- system limit, across all queues -->

 <property>
   <name>mapred.capacity-scheduler.maximum-
system-jobs</name>
   <value>3000</value>
<description>Maximum number of jobs in the
system which can be initialized,
concurrently, by the CapacityScheduler.
</description>
</property>
```

85

```xml
<!-- queue: queueA -->

 <property>
   <name>mapred.capacity-
scheduler.queue.queueA.capacity</name>
   <value>8</value>
 </property>
 <property>
   <name>mapred.capacity-
scheduler.queue.queueA.supports-
priority</name>
   <value>false</value>
 </property>
 <property>
   <name>mapred.capacity-
scheduler.queue.queueA.minimum-user-limit-
percent</name>
   <value>20</value>
 </property>
 <property>
   <name>mapred.capacity-
scheduler.queue.queueA.user-limit-
factor</name>
   <value>10</value>
 </property>
 <property>
   <name>mapred.capacity-
scheduler.queue.queueA.maximum-initialized-
active-tasks</name>
   <value>200000</value>
 </property>
 <property>
```

```xml
    <name>mapred.capacity-
scheduler.queue.queueA.maximum-initialized-
active-tasks-per-user</name>
    <value>100000</value>
 </property>
 <property>
    <name>mapred.capacity-
scheduler.queue.queueA.init-accept-jobs-
factor</name>
    <value>100</value>
 </property>

<!-- queue: queueB -->

 <property>
    <name>mapred.capacity-
scheduler.queue.queueB.capacity</name>
    <value>2</value>
 </property>
 <property>
    <name>mapred.capacity-
scheduler.queue.queueB.supports-
priority</name>
    <value>false</value>
 </property>
 <property>
    <name>mapred.capacity-
scheduler.queue.queueB.minimum-user-limit-
percent</name>
    <value>20</value>
 </property>
 <property>
    <name>mapred.capacity-
scheduler.queue.queueB.user-limit-
factor</name>
    <value>1</value>
```

```xml
  </property>
  <property>
    <name>mapred.capacity-
scheduler.queue.queueB.maximum-initialized-
active-tasks</name>
    <value>200000</value>
  </property>
  <property>
    <name>mapred.capacity-
scheduler.queue.queueB.maximum-initialized-
active-tasks-per-user</name>
    <value>100000</value>
  </property>
  <property>
    <name>mapred.capacity-
scheduler.queue.queueB.init-accept-jobs-
factor</name>
    <value>10</value>
  </property>

<!-- queue: queueC -->

  <property>
    <name>mapred.capacity-
scheduler.queue.queueC.capacity</name>
    <value>30</value>
  </property>
  <property>
    <name>mapred.capacity-
scheduler.queue.queueC.supports-
priority</name>
    <value>false</value>
  </property>
  <property>
```

```xml
    <name>mapred.capacity-
scheduler.queue.queueC.minimum-user-limit-
percent</name>
    <value>20</value>
 </property>
 <property>
    <name>mapred.capacity-
scheduler.queue.queueC.user-limit-
factor</name>
    <value>1</value>
 </property>
 <property>
    <name>mapred.capacity-
scheduler.queue.queueC.maximum-initialized-
active-tasks</name>
    <value>200000</value>
 </property>
 <property>
    <name>mapred.capacity-
scheduler.queue.queueC.maximum-initialized-
active-tasks-per-user</name>
    <value>100000</value>
 </property>
 <property>
    <name>mapred.capacity-
scheduler.queue.queueC.init-accept-jobs-
factor</name>
    <value>10</value>
 </property>

<!-- queue: queueD -->

 <property>
    <name>mapred.capacity-
scheduler.queue.queueD.capacity</name>
    <value>1</value>
```

```
  </property>
  <property>
    <name>mapred.capacity-
scheduler.queue.queueD.supports-
priority</name>
    <value>false</value>
  </property>
  <property>
    <name>mapred.capacity-
scheduler.queue.queueD.minimum-user-limit-
percent</name>
    <value>20</value>
  </property>
  <property>
    <name>mapred.capacity-
scheduler.queue.queueD.user-limit-
factor</name>
    <value>20</value>
  </property>
  <property>
    <name>mapred.capacity-
scheduler.queue.queueD.maximum-initialized-
active-tasks</name>
    <value>200000</value>
  </property>
  <property>
    <name>mapred.capacity-
scheduler.queue.queueD.maximum-initialized-
active-tasks-per-user</name>
    <value>100000</value>
  </property>
  <property>
    <name>mapred.capacity-
scheduler.queue.queueD.init-accept-jobs-
factor</name>
    <value>10</value>
```

```
    </property>

<!-- queue: queueE -->

    <property>
       <name>mapred.capacity-
scheduler.queue.queueE.capacity</name>
       <value>31</value>
    </property>
    <property>
       <name>mapred.capacity-
scheduler.queue.queueE.supports-
priority</name>
       <value>false</value>
    </property>
    <property>
       <name>mapred.capacity-
scheduler.queue.queueE.minimum-user-limit-
percent</name>
       <value>20</value>
    </property>
    <property>
       <name>mapred.capacity-
scheduler.queue.queueE.user-limit-
factor</name>
       <value>1</value>
    </property>
    <property>
       <name>mapred.capacity-
scheduler.queue.queueE.maximum-initialized-
active-tasks</name>
       <value>200000</value>
    </property>
    <property>
```

```
    <name>mapred.capacity-
scheduler.queue.queueE.maximum-initialized-
active-tasks-per-user</name>
    <value>100000</value>
  </property>
  <property>
    <name>mapred.capacity-
scheduler.queue.queueE.init-accept-jobs-
factor</name>
    <value>10</value>
  </property>

<!-- queue: queueF -->

  <property>
    <name>mapred.capacity-
scheduler.queue.queueF.capacity</name>
    <value>28</value>
  </property>
  <property>
    <name>mapred.capacity-
scheduler.queue.queueF.supports-
priority</name>
    <value>false</value>
  </property>
  <property>
    <name>mapred.capacity-
scheduler.queue.queueF.minimum-user-limit-
percent</name>
    <value>20</value>
  </property>
  <property>
    <name>mapred.capacity-
scheduler.queue.queueF.user-limit-
factor</name>
    <value>1</value>
```

```
    </property>
    <property>
      <name>mapred.capacity-
scheduler.queue.queueF.maximum-initialized-
active-tasks</name>
      <value>200000</value>
    </property>
    <property>
      <name>mapred.capacity-
scheduler.queue.queueF.maximum-initialized-
active-tasks-per-user</name>
      <value>100000</value>
    </property>
    <property>
      <name>mapred.capacity-
scheduler.queue.queueF.init-accept-jobs-
factor</name>
      <value>10</value>
    </property>

</configuration>
```

# A3) HADOOP MAPREDUCE JAVA WORD COUNT

Across all Big Data Hadoop and MapReduce that were based on the original Apache Open Source projects, a common initial first step functionality as highlighted earlier in this book include the need to parse very large files for word counts, which are more important in content and context analysis of text for semantic understanding and search engine optimization than simple byte counts are important in past storage data management optimization. Much code for such optimization of word counts were contributed to Apache Open Source for Big Data Hadoop and MapReduce. Following is a leading Java solution:

```
1. package org.myorg;
2.
3. import java.io.IOException;
4. import java.util.*;
5.
6. import org.apache.hadoop.fs.Path;
7. import org.apache.hadoop.conf.*;
8. import org.apache.hadoop.io.*;
9. import org.apache.hadoop.mapred.*;
10. import org.apache.hadoop.util.*;
11.
12. public class WordCount {
13.
14. public static class Map extends
    MapReduceBase implements
    Mapper<LongWritable, Text, Text,
    IntWritable> {
15. private final static IntWritable one =
    new IntWritable(1);
16. private Text word = new Text();
17.
18. public void map(LongWritable key, Text
    value, OutputCollector<Text, IntWritable>
    output, Reporter reporter) throws
    IOException {
19. String line = value.toString();
20. StringTokenizer tokenizer = new
    StringTokenizer(line);
21. while (tokenizer.hasMoreTokens()) {
22. word.set(tokenizer.nextToken());
23. output.collect(word, one);
24.     }
25.   }
```

```
26.   }
27.
28. public static class Reduce extends
    MapReduceBase implements Reducer<Text,
    IntWritable, Text,IntWritable> {
29. public void reduce(Text key,
    Iterator<IntWritable> values,
    OutputCollector<Text, IntWritable>
    output, Reporter reporter) throws
    IOException {
30. int sum = 0;
31. while (values.hasNext()) {
32. sum += values.next().get();
33.           }
34. output.collect(key, new
    IntWritable(sum));
35.       }
36.     }
37.
38. public static void main(String[] args)
    throws Exception {
39. JobConf conf = new
    JobConf(WordCount.class);
40. conf.setJobName("wordcount");
41.
42. conf.setOutputKeyClass(Text.class);
43. conf.setOutputValueClass
    (IntWritable.class);
44.
45. conf.setMapperClass(Map.class);
46. conf.setCombinerClass(Reduce.class);
47. conf.setReducerClass(Reduce.class);
48.
49. conf.setInputFormat
    (TextInputFormat.class);
50. conf.setOutputFormat
```

```
    (TextOutputFormat.class);
51.
52. FileInputFormat.setInputPaths(conf, new
    Path(args[0]));
53. FileOutputFormat.setOutputPath(conf, new
    Path(args[1]));
54.
55. JobClient.runJob(conf);
57.     }
58. }
59.
```

# APPENDIX B:

# ANDROID SMART PHONE CODE EXAMPLES

Nearly a decade before Apache Open Source projects were to put Big Data foundations into free licensing of basic code with permissions to modify and advance in best interest of technology worldwide, the Apache Open Source contributors and supporters had provide fundamental innovations and code foundations for the Android smart phone technology.

This was an alternative open source similar to Blackberry, Raspberry Pi and other early proprietary smart phone platforms, but Android was adapted and advanced as a preferred platform of the U.S. government and military, as well as Google and other early Cloud vendors, usually coded in C, C++, R and Python.

The following examples involve very many imports of code objects which can be found on Apache Open Source project libraries, but are useful for the novice Android coder to step through in order to get more advanced understanding of Android parameters and usage. Again, the following code is provided for instructional study purposes only, and not supported for actual builds.

## B1) APACHE ANDROID SMART CARD MAIN

The following code is from Apache Open Source Android project for smart card batch step sensor main, which involved many import libraries available on internet, which can be used in combination with Android hardware vendor smart phone functionality such as GPS.

```
/*
*
* Copyright 2013 Android Open Source Project
* Licensed under Apache License, Version 2.0
* you may not use this code except in
* compliance with the License.
*
* You may obtain a copy of the License at
*
* http://www.apache.org/licenses/LICENSE
*
* See License for language governing
* permissions and limitations under License.
*
*/

package com.example.android.batchstepsensor;

import android.os.Bundle;
import android.supp
import v4.app.FragmentManager;
import android.support.v4.app.
```

98

```
          FragmentTransaction;
import android.view.Menu;

import com.example.android.common.
       activities.SampleActivityBase;
import com.example.android.common.
       logger.Log;

import com.example.android.batchstepsensor.
       cardstream.CardStream;
import com.example.android.batchstepsensor.
       cardstream.CardStreamFragment;
import com.example.android.batchstepsensor.
       cardstream.CardStreamState;
import com.example.android.batchstepsensor.
       cardstream.OnCardClickListener;
import com.example.android.batchstepsensor.
       cardstream.StreamRetentionFragment;

public class MainActivity
   extends SampleActivityBase
   implements CardStream {

public static final String TAG =
      "MainActivity";

public static final String FRAGTAG =
           "BatchStepSensorFragment";

private CardStreamFragment
   mCardStreamFragment;

private StreamRetentionFragment
   mRetentionFragment;
```

```
private static final String RETENTION_TAG =
            "retention";

@Override

protected void onCreate(Bundle
    savedInstanceState) {
        super.onCreate(savedInstanceState);

setContentView(R.layout.activity_main);

FragmentManager fm =
    getSupportFragmentManager();

BatchStepSensorFragment fragment =
    (BatchStepSensorFragment)
    fm.findFragmentByTag(FRAGTAG);

if (fragment == null) {

FragmentTransaction transaction =
    fm.beginTransaction();

fragment = new BatchStepSensorFragment();

transaction.add(fragment, FRAGTAG);

transaction.commit();
        }

// Use fragment as click listener for cards,
but must implement correct interface

if (!(fragment instanceof
    OnCardClickListener)){
throw new ClassCastException
```

```
    ("BatchStepSensorFragment must " +
    "implement OnCardClickListener
    interface.");
            }
    OnCardClickListener clickListener =
    (OnCardClickListener)
    fm.findFragmentByTag(FRAGTAG);

mRetentionFragment =
    (StreamRetentionFragment)
    fm.findFragmentByTag(RETENTION_TAG);

if (mRetentionFragment == null) {
            mRetentionFragment = new
      StreamRetentionFragment();

fm.beginTransaction().add(mRetentionFragment
    , RETENTION_TAG).commit();
          } else {

// If the retention fragment already
existed, we need to pull some state out

CardStreamState state =
mRetentionFragment.getCardStream();

// dump it in CardStreamFragment.

mCardStreamFragment =
        (CardStreamFragment)
    fm.findFragmentById
        (R.id.fragment_cardstream);

mCardStreamFragment.restoreState
        (state, clickListener); }
    }
```

```
public CardStreamFragment getCardStream() {

    if (mCardStreamFragment == null) {
            mCardStreamFragment =
    (CardStreamFragment)
            getSupportFragmentManager()
            .findFragmentById
            (R.id.fragment_cardstream);
        }
        return mCardStreamFragment;
    }

@Override

protected void onSaveInstanceState
    (Bundle outState) {
        super.onSaveInstanceState(outState);

    CardStreamState state =
        getCardStream().dumpState();

mRetentionFragment.storeCardStream(state);
    }
}
```

## B2) APACHE ANDROID SMART SENSOR MGMT.

The following Apache Open Source project code provides example of Android smart phone standard object coding parameters and structure to integrate to Android main foundations needed to program Android compliant smart phone hardware in basic integrated applications. Notably, this code may be cumbersome to novices in C.

```
/*
*
* Copyright 2013 Android Open Source Project
* Licensed under Apache License, Version 2.0
* you may not use this code except in
* compliance with the License.
*
* You may obtain copy of the License at
*
*       http://www.apache.org/licenses/LICENSE
*
* See License for language governing
* permissions and limitations under License.
*
*/

package com.example.android.batchstepsensor;

import android.app.Activity;
import android.content.pm.PackageManager;
import android.hardware.Sensor;
import android.hardware.SensorEvent;
import android.hardware.SensorEventListener;
import android.hardware.SensorManager;
import android.os.Bundle;
import android.support.v4.app.Fragment;

import com.example.android.
       common.logger.Log;
import com.example.android.batchstepsensor.
       cardstream.Card;
import com.example.android.
       batchstepsensor.cardstream
       .CardStream;
Import com.example.android.
       batchstepsensor.
```

```
        cardstream.CardStreamFragment;
import com.example.android.batchstepsensor.
        cardstream.OnCardClickListener;

public class BatchStepSensorFragment
        extends Fragment implements
        OnCardClickListener {

public static final String TAG =
    "StepSensorSample";

// Cards

private CardStreamFragment mCards = null;

// Card tags

public static final String CARD_INTRO
    = "intro";

public static final String
    CARD_REGISTER_DETECTOR =
    "register_detector";

public static final String
    CARD_REGISTER_COUNTER =
    "register_counter";

public static final String
    CARD_BATCHING_DESCRIPTION  =
    "register_batching_description";

public static final String CARD_COUNTING =
    "counting";
```

```
public static final String CARD_EXPLANATION
    = "explanation";

public static final String
    CARD_NOBATCHSUPPORT =    "error";

// Actions from REGISTER cards

public static final int
    ACTION_REGISTER_DETECT_NOBATCHING = 10;

public static final int
    ACTION_REGISTER_DETECT_BATCHING_5s = 11;

public static final int
    ACTION_REGISTER_DETECT_BATCHING_10s = 12;

public static final int
    ACTION_REGISTER_COUNT_NOBATCHING = 21;

public static final int
    ACTION_REGISTER_COUNT_BATCHING_5s = 22;

public static final int
    ACTION_REGISTER_COUNT_BATCHING_10s = 23;

// Action from COUNTING card

public static final int
    ACTION_UNREGISTER = 1;

// Actions from description cards

private static final int
    ACTION_BATCHING_DESCRIPTION_DISMISS = 2;
```

```java
private static final int
   ACTION_EXPLANATION_DISMISS = 3;

// State of application, used to register
for sensors when app is restored

public static final int STATE_OTHER = 0;
public static final int STATE_COUNTER = 1;
public static final int STATE_DETECTOR = 2;

// Bundle tags used to store data when
restoring application state

private static final String
   BUNDLE_STATE = "state";
private static final String
   BUNDLE_LATENCY =  "latency";
private static final String
   BUNDLE_STEPS = "steps";

// max batch latency is specified in
microseconds

private static final int
   BATCH_LATENCY_0 = 0;

// no batching

private static final int
   BATCH_LATENCY_10s=  10000000;
private static final int
   BATCH_LATENCY_5s = 5000000;

/* For illustration keep track of last few
 * events and show their delay from when the
 * event occurred until received by the event
```

```
* listener. These variables keep track of
* timestamps and the number of events.
*/

// Number of events to keep in queue and
display on card

private static final int
    EVENT_QUEUE_LENGTH=10;

// List of timestamps when sensor events
occurred

private float[] mEventDelays = new
    float[EVENT_QUEUE_LENGTH];

// number of events in event list

private int mEventLength = 0;

// point to next entry in sensor event list

private int mEventData = 0;

// Steps counted in current session

private int mSteps = 0;

// Value of the step counter sensor when the
listener was registered (Total steps are
calculated from this value.)

private int mCounterSteps = 0;
```

```
// Steps counted by the step counter
previously. Used to keep counter consistent
across rotation changes

private int mPreviousCounterSteps = 0;

// State of the app (STATE_OTHER,
STATE_COUNTER or STATE_DETECTOR)

private int mState = STATE_OTHER;

// When a listener is registered, the batch
sensor delay in microseconds

private int mMaxDelay = 0;

@Override

public void onResume() {
    super.onResume();

CardStreamFragment stream = getCardStream();

if (stream.getVisibleCardCount() < 1) {

// No cards are visible, started for the
first time, Prepare all cards and show the
intro card.

initialiseCards();
showIntroCard();
```

```
// Show the registration card if hardware is
supported, show an error otherwise

        if (isKitkatWithStepSensor()) {
                showRegisterCard();
            } else {
                showErrorCard();
            }
        }
    }

@Override

public void onPause() {
        super.onPause();

// BEGIN_INCLUDE(onpause). Then unregister
the listener when the application is paused

unregisterListeners();

// END_INCLUDE(onpause)

    }

/*
* Returns true if this device is supported.
* It needs to run Android KitKat (4.4) or
* higher step counter step detect sensor.
* This check is useful when app provides an
* alternative implementation or different
* functionality if step sensor not available
* or this code runs on a platform version
* below Android KitKat. If this function is
* required, then the minSDK parameter should
* be specified in the AndroidManifest.
```

```
private boolean isKitkatWithStepSensor() {

// BEGIN_INCLUDE(iskitkatsensor)to Require
at least Android KitKat per a current SDK

int currentApiVersion =
   android.os.Build.VERSION.SDK_INT;

// Check that the device supports the step
counter and detector sensors

PackageManager packageManager =
   getActivity().getPackageManager();
    return currentApiVersion >=
   android.os.Build.VERSION_CODES.KITKAT
             &&
   packageManager.hasSystemFeature
   (PackageManager.
        FEATURE_SENSOR_STEP_COUNTER)
             &&
   packageManager.hasSystemFeature
   (PackageManager.
        FEATURE_SENSOR_STEP_DETECTOR);

// END_INCLUDE(iskitkatsensor)

 }

/*
* Handles a click on a card action.
* Registers SensorEventListener (see {@link
* #registerEventListener(int, int)}) with
* selected delay, dismisses cards and then
* unregisters listener. (see {@link
* #unregisterListeners()}).
* Actions are defined when card is created.
```

```
*
* @param cardActionId
* @param cardTag
*/

@Override

public void onCardClick(int cardActionId,
    String cardTag) {
    switch (cardActionId) {

// BEGIN_INCLUDE(onclick)
// Register Step Counter card

case ACTION_REGISTER_COUNT_NOBATCHING:

registerEventListener(BATCH_LATENCY_0,

Sensor.TYPE_STEP_COUNTER); break;

case ACTION_REGISTER_COUNT_BATCHING_5s:

registerEventListener(BATCH_LATENCY_5s,
    Sensor.TYPE_STEP_COUNTER); break;

case ACTION_REGISTER_COUNT_BATCHING_10s:

registerEventListener(BATCH_LATENCY_10s,
    Sensor.TYPE_STEP_COUNTER); break;

// Register Step Detector card

case ACTION_REGISTER_DETECT_NOBATCHING:

registerEventListener(BATCH_LATENCY_0,
    Sensor.TYPE_STEP_DETECTOR); break;
```

```
case ACTION_REGISTER_DETECT_BATCHING_5s:

registerEventListener(BATCH_LATENCY_5s,
    Sensor.TYPE_STEP_DETECTOR); break;

case ACTION_REGISTER_DETECT_BATCHING_10s:

registerEventListener(BATCH_LATENCY_10s,
    Sensor.TYPE_STEP_DETECTOR); break;

// Unregister card

case ACTION_UNREGISTER:
    showRegisterCard();
    unregisterListeners();

// reset the application state when
explicitly unregistered

mState = STATE_OTHER; break;

// END_INCLUDE(onclick)

// Explanation cards

case ACTION_BATCHING_DESCRIPTION_DISMISS:

// permanently remove the batch description
card, it will not be shown again

getCardStream().removeCard
    (CARD_BATCHING_DESCRIPTION); break;

case ACTION_EXPLANATION_DISMISS:
```

```
// permanently remove the explanation card,
it will not be shown again

getCardStream().
    removeCard
    (CARD_EXPLANATION); }

// For registered cards, display count card

if (cardTag.equals(CARD_REGISTER_COUNTER) ||
    cardTag.equals(CARD_REGISTER_DETECTOR)) {
        showCountingCards();
        }
    }

/*
*
* Register for sensor and max batch delay.
* The maximum batch delay specifies maximum
* duration in microseconds for subsequent
* sensor events can be temporarily stored by
* sensor before they are delivered to main
* registered SensorEventListener. A delay
* allows system to handle sensor events more
* efficiently, allowing system to switch to
* lower power state while the sensor is
* capturing events. Once max delay reached,
* all stored events are delivered to the
* registered listener. Note this value only
* specifies maximum delay, the listener may
* receive event quicker. Delay of 0 disable
* batch mode to register the listener in
* continuous mode.  Optimium delay depends
* on the application. Delay of 5 seconds
* or higher may be appropriate for an app
* that does not update the UI in real time.
```

```
*
* @param maxdelay
* @param sensorType
*/

private void registerEventListener(int
    maxdelay, int  sensorType) {

// BEGIN_INCLUDE(register)

// Keep track of state so correct sensor
   type and batch delay can be set up when
   app is restored (as on screen rotation).

mMaxDelay = maxdelay;

if (sensorType == Sensor.TYPE_STEP_COUNTER)
{
            mState = STATE_COUNTER;

/*
* Reset initial step counter value, first
* event received by the event listener is
* stored in mCounterSteps and used to calc
* the total number of steps taken.
*/

mCounterSteps = 0;

Log.i(TAG, "Event listener for step counter
   sensor registered with a max delay of "
   + mMaxDelay);
        } else {
   mState = STATE_ETECTOR;
```

```
Log.i(TAG, "Event listener for step detector
   sensor registered with a max delay of "
   + mMaxDelay);
        }

// Get default sensor for sensor type from
   the SensorManager

sensorManager =
   (SensorManager)

getActivity().getSystemService(Activity.
   SENSOR_SERVICE);

// sensorType is either
   Sensor.TYPE_STEP_COUNTER or
   Sensor.TYPE_STEP_DETECTOR Sensor

sensor=sensorManager.
   getDefaultSensor(sensorType);

// Register listener for this sensor in
batch mode. If the max delay is 0, events
delivered in continuous mode without batch.

final boolean batchMode =
   sensorManager.registerListener(
   mListener, sensor,
   SensorManager.SENSOR_DELAY_NORMAL,
   maxdelay);

if (!batchMode) {

// If Batch mode could not be enabled, show
warning and switch to continuous mode
```

```
        getCardStream().getCard
        (CARD_NOBATCHSUPPORT)
        .setDescription(getString
        (R.string.warning_nobatching));

getCardStream().showCard
    (CARD_NOBATCHSUPPORT);

Log.w(TAG, "Could not register sensor
listener in batch mode, " + "fall back to
continuous mode.");}

if (maxdelay > 0 && batchMode) {

// Batch mode was enabled successfully, show
a description card

getCardStream().showCard
    (CARD_BATCHING_DESCRIPTION);
        }
// Show the explanation card

getCardStream().showCard(CARD_EXPLANATION);

// END_INCLUDE(register)


    }

/*
 * Unregisters the sensor listener
 * if registered.
 */

private void unregisterListeners() {

// BEGIN_INCLUDE(unregister)
```

```
SensorManager sensorManager =
   (SensorManager)

getActivity().getSystemService
   (Activity.SENSOR_SERVICE);

sensorManager.unregisterListener(mListener);

Log.i(TAG, "Sensor listener unregistered.");

// END_INCLUDE(unregister)

    }

/*
* Resets step counter by clearing counting
* variables and lists.
*/

private void resetCounter() {

// BEGIN_INCLUDE(reset)

mSteps = 0;
mCounterSteps = 0;
mEventLength = 0;
mEventDelays = new
   float[EVENT_QUEUE_LENGTH];
mPreviousCounterSteps = 0;

// END_INCLUDE(reset)

    }

/*
```

```
* Listener that handles step sensor events
* for step detector and counter sensors.
*/

private final SensorEventListener

mListener = new SensorEventListener() {

@Override

public void onSensorChanged
    (SensorEvent event) {

// BEGIN_INCLUDE(sensorevent)to store the
delay of this event

recordDelay(event);
final String delayString = getDelayString();

if (event.sensor.getType() ==
    Sensor.TYPE_STEP_DETECTOR) {

// A step detector event is received for
each step. This means we need to count steps
ourselves

mSteps += event.values.length;


// Update card with the latest step count

getCardStream().getCard(CARD_COUNTING)
    .setTitle(getString
    (R.string.counting_title, mSteps))
     .setDescription(getString
    (R.string.counting_description,
```

```
getString(R.string.sensor_detector),
mMaxDelay, delayString));

Log.i(TAG, "New step detected by
STEP_DETECTOR sensor. Total step count: " +
mSteps);
        }

else if (event.sensor.getType() ==
    Sensor.TYPE_STEP_COUNTER) {

/*
* A step counter contains total number of
* steps since listener was first registered.
* We need to keep track of this value to
* calculate number of steps taken, as first
* value a listener receives is undefined.
*/

    if (mCounterSteps < 1) {

// initial value

mCounterSteps = (int) event.values[0];
        }

// Calculate steps taken based on first
counter value received.

mSteps = (int) event.values[0] -
mCounterSteps;
```

```
// Add number of steps previously taken,
   otherwise the counter would start at 0.
   This is needed to keep the counter
   consistent across rotation changes.

mSteps = mSteps + mPreviousCounterSteps;

// Update card with the latest step count

getCardStream().getCard(CARD_COUNTING)
   .setTitle(getString
   (R.string.counting_title, mSteps))
   .setDescription(getString
   (R.string.counting_description,

getString(R.string.sensor_counter),
mMaxDelay, delayString));

Log.i(TAG, "New step detected by
   STEP_COUNTER sensor. Total step count: "
   +  mSteps);

// END_INCLUDE(sensorevent)
          }
```

# APPENDIX C:

# ARDUINO EMBEDDED CODE EXAMPLES

More recently late in the first decade after the Apache Open Source Project for Big Data Hadoop and MapReduce, the Arduino Open Source Project was started by the original designers and developers of the Turin Italy artisans as highlighted earlier in this book.

The following examples are all included in the many hundreds of template code objects in the Arduino IDE download as previously highlighted earlier in this book. These examples are being continually updated in each new release of Arduino IDE, and are coordinated with each new release of Arduino, including new microprocessors past UNO.

Also, many newer stacker boards for each sensor type are also being continually updated between editions of this paper book. The code examples from public domain presented here are in the basic C code standard, but many other examples are being contributed daily for C++, R,

Python and others. Again, no support is provided for this code per Open Source licenses, but useful for instruction.

## C1) ARDUINO ACCELERATION SENSOR MAPS

This code sample is for a specific Arduino stacked sensor board for Analog ADXL3xx accelerometers, and the pins are specific to that board; however, it is very compatible and representative of a lot of similar boards. This same method is used as a standard template for many other Arduino sensor stacked boards using similar pins.

```
/*
 * Reads an Analog ADXL3xx accelerometer and
 * communicates acceleration to the computer.
 * The pin mappings are designed to be easily
 * compatible with boards from Sparkfun,
 * available similar to samples from:
 *
 *  http://www.arduino.cc/en/Tutorial/ADXL3xx
 *
 * This example code is in the public domain.
 */

// These constants describe static pins.

const int groundpin = 18;

// analog input pin 4 -- ground

const int powerpin = 19;

// analog input pin 5 -- voltage
```

```
const int xpin = A3;

// x-axis of the accelerometer

const int ypin = A2;

// y-axis

const int zpin = A1;

// z-axis (only on 3-axis models)

void setup()
{

// initialize the serial communications:

Serial.begin(9600);

// Provide ground and power by using analog

inputs as normal

// digital pins.  This makes it possible to
   directly connect the breakout board to
   the Arduino.  If you use normal 5V and
   GND pins on Arduino you can remove lines.

pinMode(groundpin, OUTPUT);
pinMode(powerpin, OUTPUT);
digitalWrite(groundpin, LOW);
digitalWrite(powerpin, HIGH);
}

void loop()
{
```

```
// print the sensor values:

Serial.print(analogRead(xpin));

// print a tab between values:

Serial.print("\t");
Serial.print(analogRead(ypin));

// print a tab between values:

Serial.print("\t");
Serial.print(analogRead(zpin));
Serial.println();

// delay before next input to print to log:

delay(100); }
```

## C2) ANALOG ACCELERATOR SENSOR 3D+ MAP

This Android sketch relates to multi-dimensional acceleration sensor stacker board mappings. It is for a 2-D axis map, and can be rotated virtually for 3-D+ mappings.

```
/*
*
* Read two-axis accelerometer stacker input.
* Converts output to milli-g's (1/1000
* of earth's gravity) and logs to files.
*
* http://www.arduino.cc/en/Tutorial/Memsic
*
* This example code is in the public domain.
```

```
*
*/

// these constants won't change:

const int xPin = 2;

// X output of the accelerometer

const int yPin = 3;

// Y output of the accelerometer

void setup() {

// initialize serial communications:

   Serial.begin(9600);

// initialize the pins connected to the
accelerometer as inputs:

pinMode(xPin, INPUT);
pinMode(yPin, INPUT); }

void loop() {

// variables to read the pulse widths:

int pulseX, pulseY;

// variables to contain the resulting
accelerations int accelerationX,
acceleration read pulse from x- and y-axes:

pulseX = pulseIn(xPin,HIGH);
```

```
pulseY = pulseIn(yPin,HIGH);

// accelerationX and accelerationY are in
milli-g's gravity as 1000 milli-g's, or 1g.

accelerationX = ((pulseX / 10) - 500) * 8;
accelerationY = ((pulseY / 10) - 500) * 8;

// print to log the acceleration values

Serial.print(accelerationX);

// print a tab character:

Serial.print("\t");
Serial.print(accelerationY);
Serial.println();

  delay(100); }
```

## C3) BAROMETRIC TEMP SENSOR MAPPING

This Arduino sketch is for a simple SPI standard barometric temperature sensor map. It is written by Tim Igoe, who is one of most prolific Arduino contributors.

```
/* SCP1000 Barometric Pressure Sensor on SPI
*
* Sensor attached to pins 6, 7, 10 - 13:
* DRDY: pin 6, CSB: pin 7, MOSI: pin 11
* MISO: pin 12, * SCK: pin 13
*
* By Tim Igoe - This code in public domain.
```

```
*/

// sensor communicates using SPI, so:

#include <SPI.h>

//Sensor's memory register addresses:

const int PRESSURE = 0x1F;

//3 significant bits of standard pressure

const int PRESSURE_LSB = 0x20;

//16 least significant of std temp pressure

const int TEMPERATURE = 0x21;

//16 bit temp reading for precision of all

const byte READ = 0b11111100;

// Sensor read input initialize command

const byte WRITE = 0b00000010;

// Sendot write command is initialized by
   pins used for connection with the sensor
   the other controlled by SPI library):

const int dataReadyPin = 6;
const int chipSelectPin = 7;

void setup() {
  Serial.begin(9600);
```

```
// start the SPI library:

  SPI.begin();

// initialize data ready chip select pins:

  pinMode(dataReadyPin, INPUT);
  pinMode(chipSelectPin, OUTPUT);

//Configure SCP1000 for low noise
configuration:

  writeRegister(0x02, 0x2D);
  writeRegister(0x01, 0x03);
  writeRegister(0x03, 0x02);

// give the sensor time to set up:

delay(100); }

void loop() {

//Select High Resolution Mode

writeRegister(0x03, 0x0A);

// don't do anything until ready pin high:

if (digitalRead(dataReadyPin) == HIGH) {

//Read the temperature data

int tempData = readRegister(0x21, 2);
```

```
// convert temp to celsius and display it:

    float realTemp = (float)tempData / 20.0;
    Serial.print("Temp[C]=");
    Serial.print(realTemp);

//Read the pressure data highest 3 bits:

byte  pressure_data_high =
    readRegister(0x1F, 1);
    pressure_data_high &= 0b00000111;

// only needs bits 2 max to 0 min for the
    pressure then read the data lower 16 bits

unsigned int
    pressure_data_low=readRegister(0x20, 2);

//combine two parts into one 19-bit number:

long pressure = ((pressure_data_high << 16)
    | pressure_data_low)/4;

// display the temperature:

Serial.println("\tPressure [Pa]=" +
    String(pressure));
    }
}

//Read from or write to register of sensor:

unsigned int readRegister(byte thisRegister,
    int bytesToRead ) {byte inByte = 0;
```

```
// incoming byte from the SPI

unsigned int result = 0;

// result to return

Serial.print(thisRegister, BIN);
Serial.print("\t");

// Sensor expects the register name in the
   upper 6  bits of byte. So shift bits left
   by two bits:

thisRegister = thisRegister << 2;

// now combine address command into one byte

byte dataToSend = thisRegister & READ;
Serial.println(thisRegister, BIN);

// take chip select low to select device:

digitalWrite(chipSelectPin, LOW);

// send device register you want to read:

SPI.transfer(dataToSend);

// send value 0 to read first byte returned:

result = SPI.transfer(0x00);

// decrement number of bytes left to read:

bytesToRead--;
```

```
// if you still have another byte to read:

if (bytesToRead > 0) {

// shift first byte left then get next byte:

result = result << 8;
inByte = SPI.transfer(0x00);

// combine byte you just got with last one:

result = result | inByte;

// decrement number of bytes left to read:

    bytesToRead--;
  }
// take the chip select high to de-select:

digitalWrite(chipSelectPin, HIGH);

// return the result:

  return(result);  }

//Sends write command to sensor:

void writeRegister
    (byte thisRegister, byte thisValue)      {

// Sensor still expects register address in
    upper 6 bits. So shift bits left by two:

thisRegister = thisRegister << 2;
```

```
// now combine the register address and the
   command into one byte:

byte dataToSend = thisRegister | WRITE;

// take chip select low to select device:

digitalWrite(chipSelectPin, LOW);

//Send register location

SPI.transfer(dataToSend);

//Send value to record into register

SPI.transfer(thisValue);

// take the chip select high to de-select:

digitalWrite(chipSelectPin, HIGH); } }
```

## C4) EEPROM CORE STORAGE FOR RESTART

This sketch uses an EEPROM header library which can be obtained from the Android Open Source project.

```
/*
 * EEPROM write to store for next boot.
 * Stores values read analog input 0 into the
 * EEPROM. These values stay in EEPROM when
 * the board is turned off and so they may be
 * retrieved later by another sketch.
 */

#include <EEPROM.h>
```

```
// the current address in the EEPROM

int addr = 0;

void setup()
{
}

void loop()
{

// need to divide by 4 as analog inputs
   range from 0 to 1023 and each byte of the
   EEPROM only hold a value from 0 to 255.

int val = analogRead(0) / 4;

// write value to relevant byte of EEPROM.
   These values remain when the board is
   turned off.

EEPROM.write(addr, val);

// advance to the next address.  There are
   512 bytes in EEPROM, so go back to 0 as
   start of line pointer when it hits 512.

addr = addr + 1;
  if (addr == 512)
    addr = 0;

delay(100);
}
```

# C5) ETHERNET WEB CHAT SERVER MAIN

This Arduino sketch uses an Ethernet stacker shield as highlighted earlier in this book. It uses Telnet to initialize the internet IP address, and can monitor with a display and keyboard over a serial port. It is able to connect to web or intranet on a local or remote host server, as well as an Android or other smart phone for text messaging.

```
/*
 * Chat   Server
 *
 * A simple server distributes any incoming
 * messages to all clients.  To use telnet
 * to set your device's IP address and type.
 * You can see client's input in the serial
 * monitor as well. Using Arduino Ethernet:
 * Ethernet shield links pins 10, 11, 12, 13
 * Analog inputs attaches pins A0 through A5
 *
 */

#include <SPI.h>
#include <Ethernet.h>

// Enter a MAC address and IP address for
   controller. IP address will be dependent
   on your local network. Gateway and subnet
   optional:

byte mac[] = {
  0xDE, 0xAD, 0xBE, 0xEF, 0xFE, 0xED };
IPAddress ip(192,168,1, 177);
IPAddress gateway(192,168,1, 1);
IPAddress subnet(255, 255, 0, 0);
```

```
// telnet defaults to port 23

EthernetServer server(23);
boolean alreadyConnected = false;

// whether or not client was connected prev

void setup() {

// initialize the ethernet device

Ethernet.begin(mac, ip, gateway, subnet);

// start listening for clients

server.begin();

// Open serial comm and wait for port open:

Serial.begin(9600);
   while (!Serial) { ; }

// wait for serial port to connect.

Serial.print("Chat server address:");
Serial.println(Ethernet.localIP()); }
void loop() {

// wait for a new client:

EthernetClient client = server.available();

// when client sends first byte, say hello:

   if (client) {
```

```
    if (!alreadyConnected) {

// clead out the input buffer:

client.flush();
Serial.println("We have a new client");
client.println("Hello, client!");
alreadyConnected = true; }

    if (client.available() > 0) {

// read the bytes incoming from the client:

char thisChar = client.read();

// echo the bytes back to the client:

server.write(thisChar);

// echo the bytes to the server as well:

Serial.write(thisChar);
    }
  }
}
```

## C6) ETHERNET TELNET CLIENT SERVER

This Arduino Telnet Client Server sketch uses an Ethernet stacked shield for a local host to connect to web.

```
/*
* Telnet client
* This sketch connects to a a telnet server
```

```
*
* (http://www.google.com
*
* using Arduino Ethernet shield. You'll
* need a telnet server to test this, such as
* Processing's ChatServer example (part of
* network library) works well, running on
* port 10002. It can be found in examples
* in Processing application, available at
*
* http://processing.org/
*
*/

#include <SPI.h>
#include <Ethernet.h>

// Enter MAC address and IP address for your
   controller below. The IP address will be
   dependent on your local network:

byte mac[] = {
  0xDE, 0xAD, 0xBE, 0xEF, 0xFE, 0xED };

IPAddress ip(192,168,1,177);

// Enter the IP address of the server you're
connecting to:

IPAddress server(1,1,1,1);

// Initialize the Ethernet client library
   with IP address and port of the server
   to connect to (port 23 for telnet; if
   you Processing ChatServer, port 10002):
```

```
EthernetClient client;

void setup() {

// start the Ethernet connection:

  Ethernet.begin(mac, ip);

// Open serial comm and wait for port open:

Serial.begin(9600);
   while (!Serial) { ;

// wait for serial port to connect.

   }

// give Ethernet shield 1 sec to initialize:

delay(1000);
Serial.println("connecting...");

// if a connection, report back via serial:

if (client.connect(server, 10002)) {
    Serial.println("connected");
  }
  else {

// if no connection report to the server:

    Serial.println("connection failed");
  }
}

void loop()
```

```
{

/// if incoming bytes available from the
    server, read them and print them:

if (client.available()) {
    char c = client.read();
    Serial.print(c);
  }

// as long as bytes in the serial queue,
   read and send out socket if it's open:

  while (Serial.available() > 0) {
    char inChar = Serial.read();

  if (client.connected()) {
      client.print(inChar);
    }
  }

// if server disconnected, stop the client:

  if (!client.connected()) {
    Serial.println();
    Serial.println("disconnecting.");
    client.stop();

// else do nothing to wait for disconnect:

    while(true);
  }
}
```

# C7) ETHERNET WEB SERVER MAIN

This Arduino sketch uses and Ethernet stacker shield board to provide contact to a local or remote host desktop or laptop with direct hardwire or WIFI controller access to an Internet Browser. This is 3rd of 3 sketches that can be studied together to better understand how a single Ethernet shield can be used to build 3 types of web servers.

```
/*
*
* Web Server - simple web server to show the
* value of analog input pins using Arduino
* Wiznet Ethernet shield.
*
* Ethernet shield standard attaches
* to pins 10, 11, 12, 13. Analog inputs
* for data attaches to pins A0 through A5
*
*/

#include <SPI.h>
#include <Ethernet.h>

// Enter a MAC address and IP address for
   your controller below. The IP address
   will be dependent on your local network:

byte mac[] = {
  0xDE, 0xAD, 0xBE, 0xEF, 0xFE, 0xED };
IPAddress ip(192,168,1,177);
```

```
// Initialize Ethernet server library
   with IP address and port you want to use
   (port 80 is default for HTTP):

EthernetServer server(80);

void setup() {

// Open serial comm and wait for port open:

Serial.begin(9600);
   while (!Serial) { ;

// wait for serial port to connect.

}

// start Ethernet connection and the server:

Ethernet.begin(mac, ip);
server.begin();
Serial.print("server is at ");
Serial.println(Ethernet.localIP()); }

void loop() {

// listen for incoming clients

EthernetClient client   =
server.available();

  if (client) {
    Serial.println("new client");

// an http request ends with a blank line
```

```
     boolean currentLineIsBlank = true;

    while (client.connected()) {
       if (client.available()) {
         char c = client.read();
         Serial.write(c);

// if you get to the end of the line and
   received a newline character but the new
   line is blank, the http request has
   ended, so you can safely send a reply

    if (c == '\n' && currentLineIsBlank) {

// then send a standard http response header

client.println("HTTP/1.1 200 OK");
client.println("Content-Type: text/html");
client.println("Connection: close");

// connection closed after complete response

client.println("Refresh: 5");

// refresh page automatically every 5 sec

     client.println();
     client.println("<!DOCTYPE HTML>");
     client.println("<html>");

// output value of each analog input pin

int analogChannel = 0; analogChannel < 6;

analogChannel++) {
```

```
int sensorReading =
   analogRead(analogChannel);

client.print("analog input ");
client.print(analogChannel);
client.print(" is ");
client.print(sensorReading);
client.println("<br />"); }
client.println("</html>"); break;
         }

if (c == '\n') {

// you're starting a new line

currentLineIsBlank = true; }
else
if (c != '\r') {

// you get a character on the current line

   currentLineIsBlank = false;
     }
       }
     }

// give web browser time to receive the data

   delay(1);

// else close the connection:

client.stop();
Serial.println("client disconnected");
  }
}
```

# C8) BASIC MOUSE INPUT TO ARDUINO MAIN

This is a slightly different keyboard or mouse control Arduino sketch, as it does not require additional stacker shield board, and can be implemented using a simple Arduino board such as UNO. It introduces a very basic interface to standard of all desktop computers and laptops, for mouse buttons as well as virtual mouse apps, across serial linkage from Arduino and local host computer.

```
/*
*
* KeyboardAndMouseControl - for mouse from
* virtual pushbuttons on Arduino. These 5
* are defined D2, D3, D4, D5, D6. Virtual
* mouse movement is always relative. This
* sketch first 4 buttons, and uses to set
* movement of the Arduino virtual mouse.
*
* by Tom Igoe - code is in the public domain
*
*/

// set pin numbers for the five buttons:

const int upButton = 2;
const int downButton = 3;
const int leftButton = 4;
const int rightButton = 5;
const int mouseButton = 6;

void setup() { // initialize the buttons'
inputs:
  pinMode(upButton, INPUT);
  pinMode(downButton, INPUT);
```

144

```
  pinMode(leftButton, INPUT);
  pinMode(rightButton, INPUT);
  pinMode(mouseButton, INPUT);
  Serial.begin(9600);

// initialize mouse control:

  Mouse.begin();

 Keyboard.begin(); }
void loop() {

// use serial input to control the mouse:

  if (Serial.available() > 0) {
    char inChar = Serial.read();
    switch (inChar) {
    case 'u':

// move mouse up

      Mouse.move(0, -40);
      break;
    case 'd':

// move mouse down

      Mouse.move(0, 40);
      break;
    case 'l':

// move mouse left

      Mouse.move(-40, 0);
      break;
    case 'r':
```

```
// move mouse right

    Mouse.move(40, 0);
    break;
  case 'm':

// perform mouse left click

    Mouse.click(MOUSE_LEFT);
    break;
  }
 }

// use pushbuttons to control keyboard:

  if (digitalRead(upButton) == HIGH) {
    Keyboard.write('u');
  }
  if (digitalRead(downButton) == HIGH) {
    Keyboard.write('d');
  }
  if (digitalRead(leftButton) == HIGH) {
    Keyboard.write('l');
  }
  if (digitalRead(rightButton) == HIGH) {
    Keyboard.write('r');
  }
  if (digitalRead(mouseButton) == HIGH) {
    Keyboard.write('m');
  }
 }
```

# C9) JOYSTICK 2-D INPUT TO ARDUINO MAIN

This is a similar Arduino sketch to the previous mouse example, and also based on basic functionality of the Arduino UNO microprocessor board; but is more related to control of a 2-D joystick, or virtual joystick apps.

```
/*
*
* JoystickMouseControl - Controls mouse from
* joystick on an Arduino Microchip. Uses a
* button to turn on and off mouse control,
* and second button to click left mouse for
* 2-axis joystick connect to pins A0 and A1
* pushbuttons connected to pin D2 and D3
* Virtual mouse movement is always relative.
*
* This sketch reads two analog inputs that
* from 0 to 1023 (or less on either end)then
* map translates them into ranges of -6 to 6
*
* WARNING: If you use Mouse.move() command,
* you link to a host PC yet Arduino takes
* control on mouse! Be sure you have master
* host control before you use this command!
* Fortunately this sketch includes a virtual
* pushbutton to toggle mouse control state,
* so you can turn on and off mouse control.
*
* by Tom Igoe - code is in the public domain
*
*/
```

```
// set pins for switch, joystick and LED:

const int switchPin = 2;

// switch to turn on and off mouse control

const int mouseButton = 3;

// input pin for the mouse pushButton

const int xAxis = A0;

// joystick X axis

const int yAxis = A1;

// joystick Y axis

const int ledPin = 5;

// Mouse control LED parms to read joystick:

int range = 12;

// output range of X or Y movement

int responseDelay = 5;

// response delay of the mouse, in ms

int threshold = range/4;

// resting threshold

int center = range/2;
```

```
// resting position value

boolean mouseIsActive = false;

// whether or not to control the mouse

int lastSwitchState = LOW;

// previous switch state
void setup() {
  pinMode(switchPin, INPUT);

// the switch pin

  pinMode(ledPin, OUTPUT);

// the LED pin to take control of the mouse:

  Mouse.begin(); }

void loop() {

// read the switch:

int switchState = digitalRead(switchPin);

// if changed and high, toggle mouse state:

if (switchState != lastSwitchState) {
    if (switchState == HIGH) {
      mouseIsActive = !mouseIsActive;

// turn on LED to indicate mouse state:

      digitalWrite(ledPin, mouseIsActive);
```

```
      }
   }

// save switch state for next comparison:

   lastSwitchState = switchState;

// read and scale the two axes:

   int xReading = readAxis(A0);
   int yReading = readAxis(A1);

// if mouse control is active, move mouse:

if (mouseIsActive) {
    Mouse.move(xReading, yReading, 0);
   }

// read mouse button and click or not click
   if the mouse button is pressed:

if (digitalRead(mouseButton) == HIGH) {

// if the mouse is not pressed, press it:

   if (!Mouse.isPressed(MOUSE_LEFT)) {
      Mouse.press(MOUSE_LEFT);
    }
   }

// else the mouse button is not pressed:

   else {

// if the mouse is pressed, release it:
```

```
    if (Mouse.isPressed(MOUSE_LEFT)) {
      Mouse.release(MOUSE_LEFT);
    }
  }
delay(responseDelay);
}

/*
* reads axis (0 or 1 for x or y) and scales
* analog range to arrange from 0 to <range>
*/

int readAxis(int thisAxis) {

// read the analog input:

int reading = analogRead(thisAxis);

// map reading from the analog input range
   to the output range:

reading = map(reading, 0, 1023, 0, range);

// if the output reading is outside from the
   rest position threshold, use it:

int distance = reading - center;

  if (abs(distance) < threshold) {
    distance = 0;
  }

// return the distance for this axis:

  return distance; }
```

151

# C10) WIFI WEB SERVER REMOTE SWITCH MAP

This sample Arduino sketch is specific to one particular WIFI stacker shield. However, it shows the basic programming required to perform the very most simple Arduino action – to automate a switch to blink an LED light – and as in homage to the movie 'Dodge Ball' – 'if you can blink an LED over WIFI you can switch any wireless app on and off'. Due to the obvious opportunities of this sketch as a template for great good or ill, not all of the code needed to implement this function are provided. But for instructional purposes, this is basic code taught in college.

```
/*
* WiFi Web Server LED Blink - web server
* that lets you blink an LED via the web.
* This code sketch prints IP address of WiFi
* Shield (once connected to Arduino board)
* to Serial or LED monitor. Then, you can
* open address in a web browser to turn on
* and off the LED on pin 9. Notably -
* If IP address of your shield is
* yourAddress:
*
*    http://yourAddress/H turns the LED on
*    http://yourAddress/L turns it off
*
* This example is for a network using WPA
* encryption. For WEP change Wifi.begin()
*
* by Tom Igoe - this code in public domain
*
*/
```

```
#include <SPI.h>
#include <WiFi.h>

char ssid[] = "yourNetwork";

//  your network SSID (name)

char pass[] = "secretPassword";

// your network password

int keyIndex = 0;

// your network key Index (only for WEP)

int status = WL_IDLE_STATUS;

WiFiServer server(80);

void setup() {
  Serial.begin(9600);

// initialize serial communication

  pinMode(9, OUTPUT);

// set LED pin mode for the shield:

    if (WiFi.status() == WL_NO_SHIELD) {
    Serial.println("WiFi shield
    not present");
    while (true);

// don't continue

  }
```

```
String fv = WiFi.firmwareVersion();

  if ( fv != "1.1.0" )
    Serial.println("Please upgrade
    the firmware");

// attempt to connect to Wifi network:

  while ( status != WL_CONNECTED) {

Serial.print("Attempting to connect to
    Network: ");

Serial.println(ssid);

// print the network name (SSID) then
    Connect to WPA/WPA2 network. Change this
    line if using open or WEP network:

status = WiFi.begin(ssid, pass);

// wait 10 seconds for connection:

    delay(10000);
  }
  server.begin();

// start the web server on port 80

  printWifiStatus(); }

// if connected now, print out status to log

void loop() {

  WiFiClient client = server.available();
```

```
// listen for incoming clients

    if (client) {

// if you get a client,

    Serial.println("new client");

// print a message out the serial port

    String currentLine = "";

// make String for input data from client

    while (client.connected()) {

// loop while the client's connected

        if (client.available()) {

// if there's bytes to read from the client

        char c = client.read();

// read a byte, then

        Serial.write(c);

// print it out the serial monitor

    if (c == '\n') {

// a newline character or if the
// current line is blank, end of line:
```

```
        if (currentLine.length() == 0) {

// HTTP headers start with a response code
   and content-type so the client knows
   what's coming, then a blank line:

client.println("HTTP/1.1 200 OK");
client.println("Content-type:text/html");
client.println();

// content of HTTP response follows header:

client.print("Click <a href=\"/H\">here</a>
   turn the LED on pin 9 on<br>");

client.print("Click <a href=\"/L\">here</a>
   turn the LED on pin 9 off<br>");

// The HTTP response ends with a blank line:

client.println();

// break out of the while loop:

break; }

    else {

// if you got a newline, clear currentLine:

currentLine = ""; } }
      else if (c != '\r') {

// if anything else but carriage return then

currentLine += c;
```

```
// Check to see if the client request was
   "GET /H" or "GET /L" for the HIGH-LOW
   standard test - GET /H turns the LED on
   OR GET /L turns the LED off

   if (currentLine.endsWith("GET /H")) {
      digitalWrite(9, HIGH);

   if (currentLine.endsWith("GET /L")) {
         digitalWrite(9, LOW);
      }
    }
  }

// close the connection:
   client.stop();
   Serial.println("client disonnected");
     }
  }

void printWifiStatus() {

// print SSID of network you're attached to:
  Serial.print("SSID: ");
  Serial.println(WiFi.SSID());

// print your WiFi shield's IP address:
IPAddress ip = WiFi.localIP();
  Serial.print("IP Address: ");
  Serial.println(ip);
```

```
// print the received signal strength:

  long rssi = WiFi.RSSI();
  Serial.print("signal strength (RSSI):");
  Serial.print(rssi);
  Serial.println(" dBm");

// print where to go in a browser:

Serial.print("To see this page in action,
   open a browser to http://");
Serial.println(ip);
}
```

## C11) GSM GLOBAL WEB TELEPHONE SERVER

This Arduino IDE examples sketch is for the GSM worldwide telephone web server standard that is used in Europe and around the world for the many web phone services such as Vonage and Skype among others.

This sketch uses a standard GSM Arduino stacker shield to establish an audio telephone link connection to any landline or mobile cell phone and talk either over an Arduino micro phone or cell phone such as Android to make a call based on Arduino sensor alerts and then to immediately cut over to direct phone conversation, and is a standard for most emergency communications in the world today. Again, this sketch is provided as an example for instructional purposes, and is not fully functional, but it is a good first step to understand very basic GSM coding.

```
/*
* GSM Web Server
*
* A simple web server shows the value of
* the analog input pins using a GSM shield.
*
* Circuit:
* GSM shield attached
* Analog inputs attached to
* pins A0 through A5 (optional)
*
* by Tom Igoe
*
*/

// libraries

#include <GSM.h>

// PIN Number

#define PINNUMBER ""
// APN data

#define GPRS_APN        "GPRS_APN"

// replace your GPRS APN

#define GPRS_LOGIN      "login"

// replace with your GPRS login

#define GPRS_PASSWORD   "password"

// replace with your GPRS password to
```

```
   initialize the library instance

GPRS gprs;
GSM gsmAccess;

// include parameter for debug enabled

GSMServer server(80);

// port 80 (http default) then timeout

const unsigned long __TIMEOUT__ = 10*1000;

void setup()
{

// initialize serial communications and wait
   for port to open:

Serial.begin(9600);
  while (!Serial) {
    ;
// wait for serial port to connect if Leo.

  }

// connection state

  boolean notConnected = true;

// Start GSM shield; if your SIM has PIN,
   pass as a parameter of begin() in quotes

  while(notConnected)
  {
```

```
if((gsmAccess.begin(PINNUMBER)==GSM_READY) &
        (gprs.attachGPRS(GPRS_APN,

   GPRS_LOGIN, GPRS_PASSWORD)==GPRS_READY))
      notConnected = false;

 else
    {
      Serial.println("Not connected");
      delay(1000);
    }
  }

    Serial.println("Connected to GPRS
network");

// start server

  server.begin();

//Get IP.

  IPAddress LocalIP = gprs.getIPAddress();
  Serial.println("Server IP address=");
  Serial.println(LocalIP);
}

void loop() {

// listen for incoming clients

  GSMClient client = server.available();

  if (client)
  {
```

```
    while (client.connected())
    {
      if (client.available())
      {
        Serial.println("Receiving
          request!");
        bool sendResponse = false;
        while(char c=client.read()) {

      if (c == '\n') sendResponse = true;
        }

// if you've gotten to the end of the line
   (and/or received a newline character)

      if (sendResponse)
        {

// then send a standard http response header

client.println("HTTP/1.1 200 OK");
client.println("Content-Type: text/html");
client.println();
client.println("<html>");

// output the value of each analog input pin

    for (int analogChannel = 0;
       analogChannel < 6; analogChannel++) {

client.print("analog input ");
client.print(analogChannel);
client.print(" is ");

client.print(analogRead(analogChannel));
client.println("<br />");
```

```
            }

client.println("</html>");

//necessary delay

delay(1000);
client.stop();
          }
        }
      }
    }
}
```

## C12) ARDUINO GSM SHIELD CALL TO PHONE

This Arduino sketch is very similar to the previous to make an automated alert call to an internet or intranet server, such as for purposes of an automated alert call that is coordinated over a virtual remote host or Cloud server, such as is commonly needed by 911 emergency services. This sketch uses the same Arduino GSM stacker shield board, but is more appropriate for a smaller organization, or for use by a family to notify and attempt to make phone calls to a 'short-list' for notifications, and to optionally use to call specific phone numbers worldwide from the web.

```
/*
* Make Voice Call - sketch, for the Arduino
* GSM shield, initiates a call to web phone
* or landline phone number you can enter
* through the Arduino serial monitor.
*
```

```
* To make it work, open the serial monitor,
* and when you see the READY message, type a
* phone number. Make sure serial monitor is
* set to send newline when you press enter.
* With no voice circuit the call will
* neither send nor receive any sound
*
* by Javier Zorzano
*
* This example is in the public domain.
*/

// libraries

#include <GSM.h>

// PIN Number

#define PINNUMBER ""

// initialize the library instance

GSM gsmAccess;

// include a parameter for debug enabled

GSMVoiceCall vcs;

String remoteNumber = "";

// the number you will call

char charbuffer[20];

void setup()
{
```

```
// init serial comm and wait for port open:

Serial.begin(9600);
  while (!Serial) { ;

// wait for serial port to connect if Leo

  }

Serial.println("Make Voice Call");

  // connection state

  boolean notConnected = true;

// Start GSM shield; if your SIM has PIN,
    pass it as parameter of begin() in quotes

  while(notConnected)
  {

if(gsmAccess.begin(PINNUMBER)==GSM_READY)
    notConnected = false;
  else
  {
    Serial.println("Not connected");
    delay(1000);
  }
  }

Serial.println("GSM initialized.");
Serial.println("Enter phone number ");
}

void loop()
{
```

```
// add any incoming characters to String:

while (Serial.available() > 0)
  {
    char inChar = Serial.read();

// if it's a newline, them OK to make call:

  if (inChar == '\n')
    {

// make sure phone number is not too long:

      if (remoteNumber.length() < 20)
      {

// let the user know who they are calling:
        Serial.print("Calling to : ");
        Serial.println(remoteNumber);
        Serial.println();

// Call the remote number

  remoteNumber.toCharArray
      (charbuffer, 20);


// Check if receiving end picked up the call

  if(vcs.voiceCall(charbuffer))
        {

  Serial.println("Call Established.
     Enter line to end");
```

```
// Wait for some input from the line

    while(Serial.read()!='\n' &&
    (vcs.getvoiceCallStatus()==TALKING));


// Then hang up

    vcs.hangCall();
         }
    Serial.println("Call Finished");

    remoteNumber="";

Serial.println("Enter phone number to
call.");
       }
      else
      {
Serial.println("That's too long for a phone
number. I'm forgetting it");
        remoteNumber = "";
      }
    }
    else
    {

// add last character to the message send:

    if(inChar!='\r')
        remoteNumber += inChar;
    }
  }
}
```

# BIBLIOGRAPHY

Baesens, Bart. <u>Analytics in a Big Data World: The Essential Guide to Data Science and its Applications.</u> NY: Wiley SAS Business Series (2013).

Blum, Jeremy. <u>Exploring Arduino: Tools and Techniques for Engineering Wizardry</u>. NY: Wiley (2013).

Borgman, Christine. <u>Big Data, Little Data, No Data</u>. MA: MIT Press (2015).

Cohen, Ryan and Wang, Tao. <u>GUI Design for Android Apps</u>. NY: Amazon Digital Services (2014).

Dean, Jared. <u>Big Data, Data Mining, and Machine Learning</u>. NY: Wiley (2014).

DeCapite, Donna. "Techniques in Processing Data on Hadoop". <u>Proc. of SAS Global Forum 2013</u>. Cary, NC: SAS

DiJusto, Patrick and Emily Gertz. <u>Atmospheric Monitoring with Arduino: Building Simple Devices to Collect Data About the Environment</u>. NY: Maker Media (2012).

Faludi, Robert.  Building Wireless Sensor Networks: with Arduino, XBee, and Processing.  NY: O'Reilly Media (2011).

Hammell, Bob.  Connecting Arduino: Programming And Networking With The Ethernet Shield. NY: Amazon CreateSpace (2014).

Igoe, Tom and Don Coleman and Brian Jepson. Near Field Communications with Arduino, Android, and Phone Gap Apps. NY: O'Reilly Media (2014).

Karvenin, Tero, et. al. Make Sensors: A Hands-On Primer for Monitoring the Real World with Arduino. Finland: Maker Media (2014).

Kent, Paul.  "SAS and HADOOP: The Big Picture". Proc. SAS Global Forum 2014.   Cary, NC: SAS

Little, Rod and Rubin, Don.  Statistical Analysis with Missing Data.  NY: Wiley (2014).

Magda, Yury. Arduino Interfacing and Signal Processing. NY: Amazon Digital Services (2014).

Magda, Yury.  Radio Frequency Communications in Arduino Projects. NY: Amazon Digital Services (2013).

Moors, David. "SASReduce - An implementation of MapReduce in BASE/SAS®". Proc. of SAS Global Forum 2013. Cary, NC: SAS Institute Inc.

Nielsen, Lars. Low Cost Big Data for Small to Mid Sized Firms and Lean Startups. NY: Amazon Digital Services (2014).

Schwartz, Marco. Arduino Networking. NY: Amazon Digital Services (2014).

Shajir, K. Arduino Simulation Circuits and Codes. NY: Amazon Digital Services (2014).

Simon, Phil. The Visual Organization: Data Visualization, Big Data, and the Quest for Better Decisions. NY: Wiley SAS Business Series (2014).

Rausch, Nancy and Malcolm Alexander. "Best Practices in SAS® Data Management for Big Data". Proc. of SAS Global Forum 2013. Cary, NC: SAS Institute.

www.arduino.cc/

www.aws.amazon.com/ec2/

www.azure.microsoft.com/en-us/

www.cloud.google.com/compute/

www.kickstarter.com/

# INDEX

# ABOUT THE AUTHOR

The author currently has 5 SAS V9 Certifications, including: SAS Base Programmer, SAS Statistical Business Analyst-Regression Models, SAS BI Content, SAS Platform Administration, and SAS DI Studio. He has over 30 years of experience as a SAS programmer and analyst, and has benefited from extensive SAS experience as an employee of American Airlines, Nielsen TV Ratings, JC Penney, Pepsi, Pizza Hut, KFC and, Blockbuster, to be a consultant for EPA, FDA, NASA, PHS, SSA, HCFA, CMS, among others. He has written 10+ books related to systems programming, and is currently a Senior SAS Consultant for Health Care, Finance, Operations, Big Data and Little Data Domains. More recently, he worked for Fannie Mae as a SAS architect for teams to develop ETL automation for Big Data submissions of real estate appraisal files with high volumes of financial as well as image data, and at Hewlett-Packard to prototype Hadoop and Vertica for SAS model scoring. Most recently he works as an independent consultant at **www.qualimatix.com** and is available for short projects for Hadoop and Telecommunications on Social Media mobile CRM technology using SAS. He has worked on design for several related utility patents, and participates in joint ventures and partnerships related to this emerging technologies, especially for apps for Personal Area Networks to Cloud using SAS Data Integration products. He has been an expert witness for several successful U.S. patent filings, and several personal patents pending including both provisional and non-provisional filings related to the technologies presented in this book.

## OTHER BOOKS BY THIS AUTHOR

The Peace Corps: The Early Years. ISBN: 1502795078 (Qualimatic Press, 2014).

Man-Machine Interfaces for Gyro Force Feedback. ISBN: 1502977648 (Qualimatic Press, 2014).

Dynamic Man-Machine Interfaces for NASA's V.R.. ISBN: 1502589605 (Qualimatic Press, 2014).

Dynamics of Mediation in Developmental Cognitive Affect. ISBN: 1502546736 (Qual. Press, 2014).

Windows Speech Recognition Programming API. ISBN: 0595308430 (iUniverse, 2004).

Speech Programming With Visual Basic in 21 Days. ISBN: 0595308430 (Sams/IDG, 2000).

Automated Software Performance Measurement. ISBN: 1583484604 (MultiScience Press, 1999).

Year 2000 Software Crisis Solutions for Legacy Systems. ISBN: 1583484043 (MultiScience, 1998).

Dragon Naturally Speaking Developer Guide. ISBN: 1583484043 (Intl. Thompson, 1997).

Automated Software Quality Measurement. ISBN: 0442316895 (Van Nostrand, 1994).